Book of Wisdom

Over 100 Short Stories Full of Wisdom from All Over the World

WILKAN

Table of Contents

Preface 11

I ALTRUISM 14

    The Beggar's Journey...16

    A Closet for the King...20

    Balloons...21

    The Golden Gazelle..22

    In the Village of Long Forks 25

    A Pack of Pretzel Sticks 27

    The Chess Game...28

II WEAKNESS...30

    A Single Judo Grip 32

    The Race of the Frogs..34

III PRESENCE 36

    Three Questions..38

    Where is Your Hat? 42

    The Grim Reaper 43

    Empty House 44

    The Fisherman and the Merchant 45

    Being Present..47

IV KARMA 48

    The Lotus Pond...50

    At the Market..53

    The Smart Spider..54

    Things Are Not What They Seem 56

V MATTER OF OPINION 58

Silent Debate..60

An Emperor's Dream 62

The Lucky Guy...63

Hypochondriac..65

The Cracked Bucket 66

How Poor People Live..67

The Smuggler 68

This Certainly Has Its Good! 69

The Guilty River..71

The Long Rope 72

A Good Man at the Gates of Hell 73

A Bad Request 74

Lao Tzu and the Useless Tree..75

The Decision to Save the World..76

Two Apples...77

The Book 78

Cleverly Asked 79

Answers from God..80

VI ACCEPTANCE 82

The King Cobra 84

Learn from the Earth! 86

Three Floating Robes..87

Human Nature...88

Hakuin and the Child 90

VII THANKFULNESS 92

A Hermit's Journey 94

Two Best Friends 97

In the Hammam 98

The Marbles 99

Matters of Course 100

VIII RIVALRY 102

The Mysterious Beggar Bowl 104

Three Monks 106

The Wind and the Sun 107

Three Sons 108

IX OPINIONS 110

The True Value of the Ring 112

Trying to Please Everyone 114

The Favorite Student 115

Who Knows? 116

The Mousetrap 118

The Sermon 120

The Most Delicious Vegetable in the World 121

Recession 122

The Three Sieves of Socrates 123

The Emperor's New Clothes 124

The Important Things in Life 128

X GOOD TIMES AND BAD TIMES 130

This Too Shall Pass 132

A Little Casket 135

XI ENVY 138

A Tuft of Grass and a Rose 140

The Donation 141

Two Sneaky Thieves 142

The Rich Tourist 144

Leave Traces 145

The King's Garden 146

XII ENLIGHTENMENT 148

A Well 150

Milarepa 151

The Mountain 152

An Advisor for the King 153

The Gift 154

Who Are You? 155

The Suffering Monk 156

The Diamond 157

Hakuin and a Samurai 158

Show Me Your Hate 159

The Wisdom of the Universe 160

XIII LOVE 162

Unconditional Love 164

The Perfect Woman 165

Friendship 166

The Secret Prince 168

What is Love? 169

The Brahmin and His Nephew 171

In Exile 172

XIV PERCEIVED REALITY 176

Conversation in the Womb 178

Plato's Cave 180

Allegory of the Cave by Gregory the Great..........185

Tolstoy's Parable of Reality................................186

The Temple of a Thousand Mirrors.....................187

A Disagreement of the Senses 188

What Are the People Like?................................189

The Ax Thief 190

Does God Exist? 191

Five Blind Advisors.......................................192

Good and Bad People 194

XV HOPE...196

Perseverance 198

The Goat in the Well 200

A Heavy Load...201

The Advent Wreath 202

XVI HABIT...204

The Frog in the Pot.......................................206

One Man on an Island......................................207

The Elephant in the Circus 208

The Centipede..209

About Tradition 210

XVII HUMAN EVOLUTION....................................212

The Prodigal Son 214

Two Wolves...216

Insatiability 217

Nails in the Fence 218

The Small Wave 219

Passing Through 220

Preface

This book contains 114 short stories full of wisdom for every situation in life. I grouped these stories according to subject matter, ending up with the following seventeen categories:

- ○ Altruism
- ○ Weakness
- ○ Presence
- ○ Karma
- ○ Matter of opinion
- ○ Acceptance
- ○ Thankfulness
- ○ Rivalry
- ○ Opinions
- ○ Good times and bad times
- ○ Envy
- ○ Enlightenment
- ○ Love
- ○ Perceived Reality
- ○ Hope
- ○ Habit
- ○ Human Evolution

This structure will make it easier for you, dear readers, to find the stories that are appropriate for you, depending on whatever situation you are dealing with in life so that you can draw confidence, understanding, and hope from them. These stories have the power to provide you with clarity and orientation in various life situations.

Although for the majority of the stories the sense is obvious and clear, there are also stories that must be interpreted situationally and subjectively. I have deliberately refrained from explicitly stating the meaning behind each story so that each reader is encouraged to create their own interpretations.

Most of the stories are from Buddhism and Hinduism. It is therefore not surprising that there is some focus on Asia (especially India and Japan), but this book also contains stories from Europe, Africa, and North and South America, so that wise short stories from all over the world are represented.

Despite the fact that some of the stories are of Buddhist and Hindu origin, this book has no religious focus and is aimed at everyone, regardless of religious beliefs. Many of the stories are about everyday life, and some come from famous personalities such as Lao Tzu, Plato, or Leo Tolstoy.

During my research for the book, I kept coming across the same stories, which might also already be familiar to some readers. I am sure, however, that even connoisseurs in this field can discover new stories in this collection. I am deeply indebted to the people that initiated these stories, and to those that kept them alive across generations.

I would like to conclude the preface with the summary of Mother Teresa's philosophy of life:

Life is an opportunity, avail it.
Life is a beauty, admire it.
Life is bliss, taste it.
Life is a dream, realize it.
Life is a challenge, meet it.
Life is a duty, complete it.
Life is a game, play it.
Life is costly, care for it.
Life is a wealth, keep it.
Life is love, enjoy it.
Life is mystery, know it.
Life is a promise, fulfil it.
Life is sorrow, overcome it.
Life is a song, sing it.
Life is a struggle, accept it.
Life is a tragedy, brace it.

Life is an adventure, dare it.
Life is life, save it!
Life is luck, make it.
Life is too precious, do not destroy it.

I
ALTRUISM

All the happiness in the world arises from
wanting happiness for others;

all the suffering in this world arises from
wanting happiness for oneself.

What more need be said?
The childish work for their own good;

the wise and capable for the good of others –
look at the difference between the two!

– Shantideva

The Beggar's Journey

A long time ago, a beggar lived on the street without any shelter and always had to beg for his food and drink. One day, he noticed someone was stealing his food, but he wasn't sure who it could be.

The next evening, the beggar realized that a mouse had been at his beggar's bowl. She grabbed the bread with her teeth and disappeared.

The beggar waited patiently for the mouse to return and then asked her, "Mouse, why are you stealing my food? Can't you see that I am a poor beggar? Why don't you go to the houses of the rich and take some of their food? Surely they can take it better than I can."

"Beggar, I can't explain it," replied the mouse. "But it's my job to make sure you never own more than seven things. And so I steal everything that exceeds this number from you. It is my destiny."

The mouse's words astonished the beggar. He wondered how it could be anyone's task to steal from another living thing.

The next day, when the mouse stole the bread from his bowl again, the beggar decided to find Buddha and ask him why he was only allowed to possess seven things. He packed his few belongings and left.

After a day's hike, it was getting dark. The beggar began to look around for a place to spend the night and saw a house. He knocked on the door and asked if he could spend the night. The host said yes and invited him in. The host's wife served a sumptuous meal and the beggar ate his fill for the first time in a very long time. Full of curiosity, the woman asked where the beggar was heading.

When the beggar replied that he wanted to ask the Buddha something, the woman presented him with her own request:

"When you see the Buddha, can you ask him a question for us?"

Grateful for their hospitality, the beggar agreed.

"We have a beautiful daughter," the woman began. "But she has not spoken a word since she was born. Please ask the Buddha why my daughter does not speak."

The beggar promised to ask the question and continued on his way the next morning.

After he had been on the road for several hours, he suddenly found himself facing a huge mountain range that he could not possibly cross on foot. Desperately, he searched for an alternative and soon met an old man with a long, white beard. The man held a wooden staff in his hand, at the tip of which was a yellow flickering ball enclosed by small branches.

"Are you a sorcerer?" asked the beggar.

The old man answered in the affirmative and asked what the beggar was doing so high up in the mountains.

The beggar explained that he wanted to go to ask Buddha why he had to live a life of poverty, but the mountains were blocking his way to the Buddha's temple.

The old man offered his help. "Fly with me," he said. "I will take you over the mountains."

He took the beggar by the hand and the two figures rose into the air. As they flew over the huge mountains, the sorcerer said, "Do me a favor and ask the Buddha when I will finally get to heaven. I have been waiting for one hundred years."

The beggar, who was grateful to the sorcerer for his help, promised to ask the Buddha on his behalf. After the sorcerer brought them back to earth on the other side of the mountains, the beggar continued on his way.

In the distance, the beggar could already see the temple of the Buddha, but now a huge river blocked his path. The current was so strong that he was afraid of drowning in it. The beggar settled down on the bank. To fail so shortly before the goal made him dejectedly lower his head on his chest. Gloom spread throughout him.

Then a huge turtle emerged from the river and asked him why he was so sad. The beggar told her that he was on his way to Buddha to ask him why he had to live a life of poverty.

The turtle then offered her support. "I can take you safely across the raging river," she suggested to the beggar. "In return, can you ask the Buddha when I will finally turn into a beautiful dragon? I have been waiting for a thousand years."

The beggar was grateful for the turtle's help and promised to ask Buddha her question as well.

Having crossed the river, he was finally at his destination. He went into the temple and saw the Buddha sitting in the lotus position.

He brought his hands together in wai, bowed deeply, and asked, "Venerable Buddha, I have made a long and arduous journey to meet you. May I ask you some questions?"

"Of course, you may," the Buddha replied with a smile. "You may ask me three questions."

"But I have four questions."

The Buddha was silent. The beggar pondered which question to leave out. He felt very sorry for the poor girl who had never spoken, and he asked the Buddha, "Why doesn't this pretty girl speak?"

"The girl will speak as soon as she meets her soulmate."

The beggar remembered the wise old sorcerer and decided to ask his question as well.

"The old man has only to let go of his staff, which he has been clinging to for one hundred years," replied the Buddha. "Then he will immediately ascend to heaven."

The beggar now had only one question left. When he thought of the turtle that had been waiting so long to become a dragon, his own problems seemed very small and insignificant. Therefore, he decided not to ask his own question and to ask that of the turtle instead.

"As long as the turtle hides in her shell, she will never become a dragon," the Buddha replied. "She must let go of the shell."

The beggar thanked the Buddha for his answers and left the temple. On his way back, he met the turtle and told her the Buddha's answer. The turtle slipped out of her shell and instantly transformed into a giant dragon. The dragon thanked the beggar and flew serenely into the air and away. In the shell that the dragon had left behind, the beggar found thousands of beautiful pearls from the deepest depths of the sea.

Next, the beggar met the sorcerer. He told him that he had to let go of his staff in order to go to heaven. The old man immediately let go of his staff and happily ascended to heaven.

The beggar was now rich through the pearls of the turtle and powerful through the sorcerer's staff. He flew with the staff to the house of the beautiful girl. There he told the girl's mother that her daughter would begin to speak as soon as she met her soul mate.

The daughter came down the stairs, saw the beggar, and began to speak.

A Closet for the King

The king needed a new closet, so he commissioned the best carpenter in the kingdom to make it. When the king asked the carpenter how long it would take him, he answered ten days. The king was visibly bewildered that the carpenter needed so long. Nevertheless, he commissioned him. In addition, he also commissioned a spy to watch over the carpenter as he worked.

The spy had been watching the carpenter for five days now and saw that the carpenter was not working and apparently doing nothing. It was not until the sixth day that he began to build the closet and, as promised, finished it after ten days. He had built the most extraordinary closet anyone had ever seen. The king was so pleased and curious that he called the carpenter and asked him what he had done during the first five days.

"The whole first day I spent letting go of any fears of failure or punishment if my work should displease the king. I spent the entire second day letting go of any thought that I would lack the skills to make a closet worthy of the king. The third day I spent letting go of any hope and desire for glory and reward if I were to make a closet that would please the king." The carpenter paused briefly before continuing. "I spent the whole fourth day letting go of the pride and honor that might grow within me if I were to succeed in my work and receive the king's praise. The whole fifth day I spent contemplating in my mind the clear vision of the closet that I hoped would befit a king."

Balloons

A teacher brought balloons to school and asked her students to blow them up and label them with their names. After this was done, they went to the gym together and the students put all their balloons in a pile.

The teacher mixed them up and said to the students, "Each of you needs to find your own balloon again. You have five minutes to do this." The students got straight to the task, but only a few found their balloons. Most searched in vain until the time ran out.

Next, the teacher asked her students to each grab a balloon and hand it to the student whose name was on it. It wasn't a minute before each child was holding their own balloon in their hands again.

"These balloons represent happiness," the teacher said. "If we only look for our own, we will never find it. But if we care about other people's happiness, we will find our own."

The Golden Gazelle

In one of his many lives, Siddhartha Gautama was a gazelle. When he came out of the womb, he shone like gold, his eyes sparkled like diamonds, and his horns were the color of silver. The golden gazelle was called *Tejas* and was the king of two hundred gazelles whose home was the forest. Near them lived another herd of two-hundred gazelles. Their king, *Sakha*, also had a golden coat.

The King of Men, Raj, loved to hunt. Every day he hunted animals and ate their meat. His subjects were exhausted from the intense daily hunting excursions. Therefore, they lured the two herds of gazelles into the royal park and confined them there. Four hundred gazelles, with their two kings Tejas and Sakha, were now in captivity.

When King Raj entered the park, he immediately noticed the two golden gazelles. He ordered that these two special creatures were not to be hunted under any circumstance. Instead, Raj and his cook killed one of the other gazelles every day. Every day there was great suffering when the hunters came to take one of the gazelles. The animals panicked and tried to escape, and many were injured by arrows during the hunt until finally one gazelle was killed.

Sakha then went to Tejas and made the following suggestion.

"We are living in terrible times," he began. "Our folk is suffering a lot. How would it be if every morning an animal would voluntarily sacrifice itself? Which gazelle it will be will be decided by lot, and it shall alternate between a gazelle from your herd and one from mine. The unfortunate gazelle would then go to an agreed place and sacrifice itself for the herd."

"This is how we will do it," Tejas replied. "Even though many would die, we can avoid unnecessary pain by doing so."

This proposal also pleased King Raj, and so they proceeded until one day the lot fell upon a pregnant gazelle from the herd of Sakha. She went to her king and asked for parley.

"My king, I am carrying a child," she spoke. "If I have to sacrifice myself, then two of us will die right away. Please let the lot pass me by this time."

However, Sakha refused the request. "I cannot help you. The lot has decided. You know what you have to do."

In her hopeless situation, the pregnant gazelle turned to Tejas and complained to him about her suffering.

He did not think long before saying: "You shall be free. I will sacrifice myself to the king today."

He went to the appointed place, where the cook was already waiting. However, when he saw the golden gazelle, he could not believe his eyes. *How is it that Tejas himself appears at the place of sacrifice? The king ordered that the golden gazelle should not be killed under any circumstances.* The cook then rushed to the king and told him about it.

King Raj was astonished. He wanted to see for himself and went to the royal park. When he arrived there, he caught sight of Tejas.

"Tejas, why are you in the place of sacrifice?" asked the king of men in amazement. "You are under my personal protection and I will not let you be killed."

"Today the lot fell on a pregnant gazelle. She begged me to be spared for the sake of her unborn baby. Because I do not want to inflict the suffering of death upon others, I came here. I am ready to sacrifice my life for her and her unborn child."

Raj thought silently for a while before responding. "I have never met anyone like you, Tejas. Your charity has defeated me. I grant freedom to you and that pregnant gazelle."

"If we are both free, what happens to our brothers and sisters here in the park? They, too, want to live in freedom."

"They, too, shall live in freedom. I release you all back into the forest."

"And what about the other gazelles in the kingdom that live in the forest?"

"They too shall live a free life without worry."

"But what about the other animals, the birds, and the fish? How will they fare?"

"Much the same. They have nothing more to fear from me."

In this way, Tejas achieved freedom for all animals in the kingdom. In the royal court, there was no more hunting and life was spared.

In the Village of Long Forks

There once lived a man who traveled the world. He had already experienced a lot on his countless journeys. So it happened that one day he came across a lone house. Far and wide there were no other buildings in sight, but on the front door was written, "Welcome to the village of long forks."

All of this made the traveler curious, so he decided to enter the house. Inside, he saw that the hallway divided the house into two halves. "This way to the black village of the long forks" was written on a blackboard nearby, along with "This way to the white village of the long forks," with arrows indicating the directions.

The traveler decided to first visit the black village of the long forks. He walked down the long corridor and came to a closed door, behind which he heard wailing and groaning. Fearful but curious, he slowly opened the door. Inside the room, many people were sitting at a large table covered with the most marvelous food. It smelled delicious and the table almost arched under the weight of the numerous dishes. Upon closer inspection, the traveler was startled. People were tied to their chairs with their bodies, arms, and legs. Long-handled forks were tied to their wrists. These were so long that they could not manage to put even a single bite into their mouths. The people were not able to feed themselves and were near starvation.

Filled with horror, the traveler quickly closed the door and briskly headed for the white village of long forks. When he arrived there, he heard merry laughter and chatter behind the door. The mood was audibly positive. When he opened the door, he was met with a similar picture as before. Again, people were sitting at a large table lavishly covered with all kinds of food. It smelled just as delicious as in the room before, and again the table almost bent under the weight of the food. And, just as in the black village of the long forks, here too people were tied to their chairs and had long-handled forks tied to their wrists, with which they could not possibly reach their own mouths.

But how was it that they nevertheless all sat together in such high spirits? That's when the traveler observed: they fed each other.

A Pack of Pretzel Sticks

A woman just missed her train and the next one wouldn't arrive for another hour. She went to the nearby newsstand and bought a newspaper and a pack of pretzel sticks. In the crowded waiting area, she sat down next to a man and started reading her newspaper. As she did so, she ate the pretzel sticks.

After a while, she noticed that the man, who was reading a book, was also helping himself to her pretzel sticks. The woman was outraged but she didn't want to make a scene out of it. She pretended that nothing had happened, continued reading her newspaper, and nibbled the pretzel sticks one by one. The man did the same – he also ate one pretzel stick after the other. This made the woman furious. Inside, she was seething with rage. But she didn't want to start a fight in the crowded waiting area and tolerated the man's insolent behavior.

When only one pretzel stick remained in the package, the man took it, broke it into two equal halves and, without looking at the woman, gave one half to her. The woman took half of the pretzel stick but was furious at the man's audacity. She pulled herself together, folded up her newspaper, and got up to leave the waiting area.

When she went to put her newspaper in her bag, she noticed an unopened package of pretzel sticks in her pocket. Then she realized that she had been helping herself to the man's pretzel sticks all along.

The Chess Game

A woman came to a nearby monastery and met the head monk. "I am dissatisfied with myself and my life," she told him. "I have read a lot about the spiritual path. Therefore, I have decided to attain enlightenment in order to be liberated from suffering. But I can't concentrate for a long time. Besides, I want to make progress quickly. Is there a shorter path for people like me?"

"There is. But only if you are truly determined." The monk paused briefly before continuing. "But first, tell me what have you focused on most in your life."

After pondering a bit, the woman replied, "My great passion used to be playing chess. I spent many hours playing it."

The monk asked the woman to wait a moment. He left and returned a few moments later, accompanied by another monk who had a chessboard with him. He began to set up the pieces. The head monk also brought a sword.

"You two will now play a game of chess against each other," he ordered the woman and the monk. "The loser will pay with their life. But I promise that the loser will end up in heaven."

The woman and the monk immediately saw that the head of the monastery was serious about his threat.

The chess game began. During the opening moves, the woman felt sweat running down her forehead as she played for her life. The chessboard became her whole world – she was completely focused on it and no longer perceived anything around it.

At first, the monk had the better position and quickly gained the advantage. But then he made a bad move and the woman captured his rook. The monk's position was shaken. The woman looked at her opponent and saw the face of a virtuous and intelligent man, marked by years of rigorous effort. As she compared his life with hers, a wave of compassion came over her. Deliberately, she began to make mistakes one by one so that the monk could win the game. Suddenly, the head of the monastery intervened. He overturned the chessboard before the game could be finished. The woman and the monk were startled and amazed at the action of the head of the monastery.

"There is no winner and no loser in this game," he explained. "Nor will anyone have to die today because of it." Turning to the woman, he continued, "Only two things are required: complete concentration and altruism. You learned both today. You were completely focused on the game and yet you were able to feel compassion. So much so that you were willing to sacrifice your life for another. You can stay in the monastery and begin your first steps toward enlightenment here."

II
WEAKNESS

With a bit of skill you can build a stairway with the stones that are put in your way.

– Chinese wisdom

A Single Judo Grip

A boy was born without his right arm. At the age of ten, he became interested in sports and was particularly curious about judo. The boy took lessons from a successful judo master. He enjoyed the training and made great progress. What he did not understand was why, after several months, the master had still only taught him one grip.

"Master, shouldn't I learn more grips?" the boy asked.

"That's the only grip you will ever need to know."

The boy did not understand the answer, but he had full confidence in his master and continued to train this one grip.

Months passed and the boy participated in a tournament for the first time. To his and the spectators' astonishment, he won the first two fights without much effort. As the rounds went on, the skill of his opponents increased, but he made it to the finals. He won all his fights with his single grip. After all, he did not know any others.

In the final, he faced a boy who was taller, older, and stronger than him. Not only did the other boy have both of his arms. He also had more tournament experience. The referee expressed his concerns about the unfair fight and wanted to cancel it. He was worried that the one-armed boy would be seriously injured. The boy also doubted his chances of defeating this opponent. But the master insisted on the fight.

The fight began. At first, it seemed that the disadvantaged boy had no chance. But in a moment of his opponent's carelessness, the boy managed to apply his only grip – and with it, to the astonishment of all, he won both the fight and the tournament.

On the way home, the student and master went through all the fights and analyzed them.

"Tell me, master, how was it possible that I could win the tournament with only one grip?" the student asked.

"There are two reasons for that," the master replied. "First, the grip you have mastered is one of the most difficult and best grips in judo. And secondly, the only way to defend against it is to grab your opponent's right arm."

The Race of the Frogs

One day, many frogs decided to organize a race. To make it extra difficult, they set the finish line at the highest point of a big tower. On the day of the race, the spectating frogs took their places and the participating frogs went to the starting line. The unanimous opinion among the spectators was that none of the frogs would reach the finish line. The race began.

Instead of cheering on the participating frogs, the spectators only bawled. "You'll never make it!" "That's impossible!" or "You won't make it anyway!" were the remarks that could be heard.

At first, it seemed that the spectators' opinion was true. Gradually, more and more of the participating frogs gave up.

The demotivating shouts continued unabated.

"Oh dear, those silly things! They won't make it to the finish line anyway!"

In the meantime, all the frogs – except for one – had given up. The last frog continued to climb the steep tower undeterred. It was exhausting and he struggled to reach the goal. The spectators observed this and shouted to him that it was impossible and that he had better give up before he fell down the tower.

But the frog continued to fight. Yard by yard. Until ... finally! He reached the finish line and won the race.

After his victory, he took the stairs down and met one of the other participating frogs, who asked him how he did it. But the winner did not answer.

And then the other found out: the winning frog was deaf!

III
PRESENCE

You can't think about presence,
and the mind can't understand it.
Understanding presence is being present.

– Eckhart Tolle

Three Questions

Leo Tolstoy once wrote of an emperor who believed that if he knew the answer to three questions, he could never be wrong again.

The three questions were:
1. What is the right time to do something?
2. Which people are the most important to care for?
3. What is the most important thing to do?

He asked these questions to all the sages and scholars of his kingdom. He promised that the person with answers that satisfied him would be richly rewarded. But the sages and scholars told the king that the questions could not be answered precisely, while some gave answers that did not satisfy the king. Therefore, no one received a reward.

The emperor then decided to seek out a hermit, who was said to have attained enlightenment, to ask him the three questions.

The hermit lived in a mountain cave and was known for helping poor people. He hardly ever encountered rich and powerful people. Therefore, the emperor disguised himself as a simple peasant. He ordered his entourage to wait for him at the foot of the mountain while he made his way to the hermit.

When the emperor arrived, the hermit was in the process of planting a garden. The hermit saw the emperor in disguise, nodded to him, and continued digging.

"I have come to you because I want to know the answers to my three questions," the emperor said. "What is the right time to do something? Which people are the most important to care for? And what is the most important thing to do?"

The hermit heard the emperor's words but gave no reply and continued to dig.

The emperor saw the elderly hermit's exhaustion. "You must be tired," he observed. "Let me help you."

The hermit thanked him, gave him the spade, and sat down to rest. After two hours of gardening, the emperor asked the hermit his three questions again. The latter stood up and said, "I am now rested and can continue. You can rest now." But the emperor refused and continued digging.

In the meantime, the sun had set when the emperor turned to the hermit again. "I have come to you for answers to my three questions. If you don't have any answers for me, just tell me and I'll be on my way home again."

Again the hermit gave the emperor no answers to the questions asked but instead asked his own question. "Do you hear someone running over there?"

A man emerged from a patch of woods and ran toward them. He held both hands pressed to his stomach and was bleeding profusely. In front of the emperor, the man fell to the ground unconscious. The emperor saw a deep abdominal wound, which he cleaned and bandaged with his own shirt. Because it immediately became soaked with blood, he wrung out the shirt and bandaged the wound again. He repeated this until the bleeding stopped. When the man regained consciousness, he asked for water. The emperor hurried to the stream and gave the man something to drink.

After this exhausting day, they spent the night together at the hermit's house.

The next morning the man looked at the emperor and said, "Forgive me."

"What have you done that I should forgive you?" asked the emperor in irritation.

"You do not know me, Your Majesty, but I know you," the man began to explain. "In the last war, you killed my brother and took my property. When I found out that you would come alone to the hermit, I decided to kill you here. However, your servants recognized me and inflicted the wound on my stomach. I escaped at the last second and came here, where you fortunately saved my life. I was planning to kill you and now you have saved my life instead. I am deeply ashamed and would like to thank you from the bottom of my heart."

The emperor was overjoyed at how easily he could reconcile with his former enemy. He not only forgave the man but he promised to return his property to him.

In the meantime, the emperor's servants had arrived and were standing in front of the hermit's cave. The emperor ordered them to take the wounded man home, where his personal physician would give him medical attention. Before the emperor began his journey back, he turned to the hermit once more, asking him to answer his three questions.

The hermit looked kindly at the emperor. "But your questions have already been answered," he stated.

"Is that so?" asked the emperor in amazement.

The hermit nodded. "If you hadn't taken pity on me yesterday and helped me with the gardening, the man would have ambushed you on the way back. Then you would have deeply regretted not staying with me. So the right time was the time when you helped me with the gardening. The most important person was me. The most important thing was to help me."

The emperor stumbled when the hermit's words became clear to him.

"Later, when the wounded man came running here, the most important thing was the time you spent bandaging his wound. Because otherwise the wounded man would have died and you would have failed to reconcile with him. So, as before, the most important person was the wounded man and

the most important thing was to take care of his wounds."
The hermit looked urgently at the emperor. "Remember:
there is only one important time and it is now! The present
moment is the only time we have at our disposal. The most
important person is always the one we are with right now.
And the most important thing is to make the person by our
side happy."

Where is Your Hat?

An adept's chela has lived in seclusion for six months, meditating most of his time. Then the time had come to return to his teacher. The chela was looking forward to seeing his teacher again. In the past months, he had collected some questions to ask the adept.

Before entering the hut, the chela took off his hat. He bowed to his teacher, expecting a conversation about his unanswered questions. He wanted to know whether the universe is finite or infinite; what is beyond duality; how universes come into being and pass away; what was the very first cause; and much more.

After greeting him, the adept asked, "Where is your hat?"

"I left it in front of the hut."

"How did you put it down?"

"I hung it on one of the nails."

"On which of the nails exactly? The left nail, the middle nail, or the right nail?"

The chela was visibly irritated that the adept asked such unimportant questions. "I don't know," he replied. "I was thinking of the questions I want to ask you."

"Go away again," the adept said, "and meditate for another six months before returning to me."

The Grim Reaper

A man had somehow managed to make friends with the Grim Reaper. He asked to be warned in time when his time had come and the Grim Reaper agreed to this request.

Years passed. The Grim Reaper came to his friend and said, "Tomorrow is the day I will take you away."

"Are you serious?" the man asked, upset. "You promised to give me plenty of notice, didn't you?"

"But I gave you many signs," replied the Grim Reaper. "You just failed to notice them. When your mother died, you didn't know how to interpret my sign; when your father died, you didn't recognize that sign; when I took your brother, your neighbor, and your aunt one by one, you closed your eyes. And tomorrow I'm coming for you."

When the Grim Reaper picked up the man the next day and led him into the afterlife, they passed many people who had already died and who shouted loudly, "Grim Reaper, why didn't you let us know in time? There was so much we could have done before!"

The Grim Reaper turned to his friend and told him, "Do you see how people are dealing with my signs?"

Empty House

In a Siberian village lived an old Babushka. On one stormy winter night, she had already made herself comfortable under the blankets and was about to fall asleep when there was a knock at the door. She wondered who could possibly be outside in such a storm and was reluctant to leave her bed. But the knocking did not stop, and so Babushka went to the door.

When she opened the door, she saw two excited men. "Come quickly, Babushka," one of the men called excitedly. "A child has just come into the world, just down the street. Your experience is needed so you can bless the child and the new parents."

"I'll be there tomorrow," Babushka replied. She longed for her cozy bed and had no desire to go to the child in the stormy weather.

Shortly after the two visitors left, there was another knock at the door. When Babushka opened the door this time, there was a woman standing in front of her, begging for a basket. She asked Babushka to give her some blankets for the newborn child. But this time, too, Babushka put off the visitor until tomorrow.

The next day the storm had subsided and Babushka was rested. She packed her basket with food, clothes, and a few blankets for the child and parents and walked down the snow-covered street. Arriving in front of the house, however, she found that the house was empty. No one was there anymore.

The Fisherman and the Merchant

Early in the morning, a fisherman took his boat out to sea to cast his fishing nets. Later, having caught his catch for the day earlier than usual, he returned to the harbor, looking forward to finishing his work. At the same time, a merchant was walking along the boardwalk during his lunch break and saw the fisherman docking his boat.

"Why don't you want to set out into the sea again to catch more fish? The day is still young," the merchant asked after observing the fisherman for a bit.

"Oh, you know," the fisherman replied, "I have a lot of things to do today. I want to spend some time with my children and my wife. In the evening, my wife and I want to go to the theater with friends. Then I would like to spend the rest of the evening in my rocking chair in the garden in peace and quiet with a cup of tea and just do nothing."

"Yes, but if you would just work a few hours more every day, you would catch more fish," the merchant argued. "As a result, you would earn more and could put your surplus money aside. After some time, your extra financial cushion should be enough to buy a bigger fishing boat, with which you would catch even more fish." The merchant made a hand gesture and pointed to the boat. "You could then sell the larger amount of fish through a wholesaler and not have to do it yourself at the market stall. That way you could retire earlier."

"And what would I do then if I were to retire early?"

The merchant thought for a moment before answering. "Well," he began hesitantly, "you could spend time with your family and friends. You could go to the theater or spend evenings in the garden with a hot cup of tea. In addition, of course, you would still have the time to sail your boat into the sea in the morning to catch fish."

The fisherman smiled before calmly replying. "But that's exactly what I'm doing right now."

Being Present

Near a village lived an old sage known for being happy and serene. Some young men came to him to ask about the secret of his happiness.

"Sage, how is it that you are always so happy and serene? Please teach us to be so happy and serene, too." "What is your secret?" The young men's questions and requests were many.

"When I lie down, I lie down. When I sit, I sit. When I walk, I walk, and when I eat, I eat," the sage replied.

The young men looked at each other, confused.

"That's what we do, we lie, sit, walk and eat. Why aren't we happy? After all, we are doing exactly the same thing," said one of them.

"When I lie, I lie. When I sit, I sit. When I walk, I walk, and when I eat, I eat," the sage repeated his answer.

The young men still did not understand the statement and looked at each other again.

"Yes, you also do all these things," the sage confirmed. "You lie, you sit, you walk, you eat. But while you are lying down, you are already thinking about sitting. While you are sitting, you are already thinking about walking. While you are walking, you are already thinking about your arrival. While you are eating, you are already thinking about drinking. Because of this, your thoughts are constantly somewhere else and not where you are. Life takes place only in the here and now. Let yourself be in this moment and you too have the chance to be truly happy and serene."

IV
KARMA

Watch your thoughts,
for they become words.

Watch your words,
for they become actions.

Watch your actions,
for they become habits.

Watch your habits,
for they become your character.

Watch your character,
for it becomes your destiny.

– From the Talmud

The Lotus Pond

The Tathagata once told of a beautiful lotus pond. Not a single fish lived in this pond. But not far from this pond there was a smaller pool, which was home to many fish, crabs, and a single crayfish.

One day a heron came flying over the pool and noticed the cramped living space of the fish and crabs. He devised a plan, landed at the edge of the water, and made a sad face.

"Why are you making such a sad face? What is worrying you?" asked the fish and crabs.

"It is because of you that I am so sad," replied the heron. "Your pool is muddy and stinks. You lack good food. I feel very sorry for you and your hard life."

"Do you know any way to help us?" asked a fish.

"Yes, I do. There is a lotus pond very close by. I could take you there one by one and set you down in the fresh, cool water. There is also plenty of room and food for all of you."

The fish and crabs, however, were skeptical. "We'd like to believe you, but we've never heard of herons caring about the fate of fish or crabs. You're just trying to trick us so you can eat us, aren't you?"

"Why are you so suspicious? Deceiving you is not in my interest. The lotus pond really exists. I can prove it to you. Let me fly one of you over there so he can see for himself. Afterward, I will fly him back and he can report to you whether I have told the truth or not."

The fish and crabs consulted for a while. They agreed to allow one of the older fish to fly with the heron. This fish was a skillful swimmer who could also move on sand. The heron took the fish in his beak and flew with him to the lotus pond. Once there, he set the old fish down in the water and let him explore the pond. And it was indeed as the heron had promised – the pond was large, cool, refreshing, and provided plenty of food for the fish and crabs. When the heron brought him back to the small pool, the fish described everything he had seen.

The fish and crabs were now persuaded of the heron's good intentions and asked him to fly them over to the lotus pond. And so the heron took a fish in his beak and flew away. But this time their destination was not the pond, but the Plumeria tree. He perched on a branch of the tree and ate the fish, letting the bones fall to the ground when he was finished. He flew back to get the next fish and ate that one, too. For several days, he kept collecting new fish to eat. Finally, when he had eaten all the fish, he began to eat the crabs in the same way. The pile of bones and shells by the tree trunk was already huge.

When the heron had also eaten all the crabs, only the single crayfish remained. "Now all the fish and all the crabs are in the lotus pond, where they live happily," the heron stated, addressing the crayfish. "Don't you want me to fly you there too?"

"How do you want to carry me?" asked the crayfish.

"The way I carried the fish and crabs, in my beak."

"What if I slip out of your beak and fall down? Then I would surely die."

"Don't worry," the heron tried to reassure him, "I will fly very carefully."

The crayfish thought for a while and then devised a plan. "I'm not sure if your beak is strong enough to hold me tightly. I'll come along if I can clasp your neck with my claws. That way I can hold on while flying."

The heron accepted the condition and they flew off. But instead of setting the crayfish down in the cool water, the heron landed on the branch of the plumeria tree, just as before.

"Why are you putting me down here and not in the lotus pond?" the crayfish asked in wonder.

"Which heron is so stupid as to bring fish to a lotus pond?" the heron replied sarcastically. "I am not your helper. Here I ate all the fish and crabs, and here I will eat you, too."

"The fish and crabs may have been easy to fool, but not I. Either you take me to the lotus pond right now, or I'll cut your head off with my claws!" The crayfish began to make good on its threat and dug its sharp claws deeper into the heron's neck.

Tormented by intense pain, the heron screamed. "That hurts! Don't grip so hard! Fine. You won; I'll take you to the lotus pond immediately."

The heron flew to the lotus pond to drop the crayfish there. But the crayfish did not loosen its grip on the heron's neck. While flying, the crayfish could only think of the terrible fate of the fish and crabs. He dug his claws deeper and deeper into the heron's neck until he had severed it completely. The heron fell dead to the ground and the crayfish crawled into the water of the pond.

At the Market

A woman went to a market. There she saw a man who had a stall but no goods.

"What are you selling?" she asked the vendor.

"Everything God has to offer."

The woman was completely stunned and thought about what to buy. Finally, she seized the opportunity and said, "I want to be happy; I want peace and love for my soul. I want to be free from fear and, moreover, I want to be in possession of absolute wisdom." Then she added, "But I want all this not only for myself but for all of humankind."

The man packed up a small package and handed it to the woman.

The woman looked at the salesman in irritation as she weighed the small package in her hand. "Is this all?" she asked incredulously.

The man smiled and replied, "Dear lady, the store of God does not sell fruit, only seeds."

The Smart Spider

A fire was raging in the African savannah. All the animals were frightened and ran around frantically. An antelope, almost trapped by the fire, had nearly lost hope of finding an escape route when it suddenly heard a soft voice.

"Let me climb into your ear so that we can escape together." It was the voice of a spider named Shari.

Without even waiting for the antelope's response, she immediately jumped off the branch into the antelope's ear. Shari knew the escape route and guided the antelope out of the life-threatening place. The antelope hopped over bushes and shrubs, crossed the undergrowth, and jumped over streams. When the fire was far away, the spider climbed onto the ground.

"Thank you for saving me," she said to the antelope. "I hope we will meet again someday. Because, as the saying goes, you always see each other twice in life."

Months passed, and the antelope gave birth to a calf. The latter spent the first days of life in the dense bushes for protection, while the mother grazed in the pasture. After a few weeks, mother and child were grazing together when two hunters spotted the two antelope. The calf quickly hid in the bushes while the mother jumped around to divert their attention. She succeeded: the hunters gave chase and the calf stayed behind

On foot, the hunters could not keep up the pursuit for long. They decided to return and at least finish off the calf. But their search was in vain. And so they left the area without prey.

When the antelope returned, she did not find her child in the usual hiding place. Panic-stricken, she began to search for her child until she heard a familiar voice. It was the spider Shari, who led her into a thicket enveloped by a dense spider web. Underneath, almost invisible, lay the calf.

While the mother lured the hunters away, Shari diligently wove cobwebs and successfully hid the calf from the hunters.

Things Are Not What They Seem

An angel and an archangel were on a journey together. The sun had already set and they stopped to spend the night with a wealthy family. However, the family was rude and refused the two guests their guest room. Instead, they were to spend the night in a cold, damp cellar.

As the angel lay down to sleep on the floor, he watched the archangel resealing a hole in the wall. He asked him about it and the archangel replied, "Things are not always what they seem."

They spent the whole next day on their feet and because it had already become late, they looked around again for a place to stay. There they met a poor family that was happy to take them in. The hosts shared their food with the angels and even let them sleep in their bed. They themselves spent the night on the sofa in the living room.

The angels woke up after a restful night and found their hosts in tears. Their only cow, on whose milk they relied, lay dead in the field.

"Why did you let this happen?" the angel angrily asked the archangel. "The rich family had everything and yet you helped them. Now, with the poor family, you let the cow die."

"When we were resting in the cold cellar, I noticed that there was gold in that hole in the wall. Because the hosts were so greedy and didn't want to share their possessions, I sealed the wall so they couldn't find it. Last night, as we slept in the poor family's bed, the Grim Reaper came for the wife. I gave him the cow instead." The archangel looked at the angel urgently before repeating, "As I said, things are not always what they seem."

V
MATTER OF OPINION

If a stone thought, "A single stone cannot raise a wall," there would be no buildings.

If a grain of wheat thought, "A single grain of wheat cannot sow a field," there would be no harvest.

If a drop of water thought, "A single drop of water cannot form a puddle," there would be no seas.

If a sunbeam thought, "A single sunbeam cannot brighten a day," there would be no light.

If human beings thought, "A single gesture of love has no influence on humankind," there would be no love in the world.

– Unknown

Silent Debate

In a Buddhist temple, any traveling monk could settle for a short time if he had a debate about Buddhism with a resident monk and won. However, if he lost, he had to move on. There were two brother monks living in such a temple. The older one was well-educated, while the younger one had only one eye and was feeble.

One day, a traveling monk came to the temple and intended to settle for a few days. He challenged the elder brother. The latter, however, had been studying the Upanishads all day and was exhausted. He then asked his brother to conduct the debate in his stead. He also wanted the debate to be done silently.

The traveling monk accepted the conditions. He and the brother went to a suitable room. The debate ended rather quickly and the traveling monk went to the elder brother.

"Your younger brother is a splendid fellow," he announced to the older brother. "He has defeated me."

The elder brother wanted to know how the debate went.

"Well, first I held up a finger," the traveling monk began to tell. "The finger that represents *Buddha – the enlightened one.* Then he held up two fingers, indicating Buddha and his teaching. I held up three fingers, representing Buddha, his teaching, and his followers living in harmony." The traveling monk paused for a moment before continuing. "Thereupon your younger brother punched me in the face with his fist, indicating that all three come from one realization. Thus he won. And I have no right to settle here for a few days."

No sooner had the traveling monk left the temple than the younger brother came rushing in.

"Where is that guy?" he asked angrily.

"Why are you so upset?" the older brother countered. "I guess you won the debate?"

"Not in the least. I'm going to beat him up."

The older monk asked his brother to tell him how the debate went.

"Well," the younger brother began to explain, "no sooner did we sit down than he raised a finger and insulted me."

The older brother did not understand at first, but the younger one immediately went on.

"With that, he alluded to the fact that I only have one eye. Since he was a stranger, I wanted to be polite to him. I held up two fingers, congratulating him on having two eyes. Thereupon the rude lout then held up three fingers. He wanted to illustrate to me that we would only have three eyes when put together. That's when I blew a fuse and I punched him in the face. He then ran out of the room and our debate ended."

An Emperor's Dream

The emperor was jolted out of sleep at night by a nightmare. He immediately called for a dream reader and told him about his dream.

"In my dream, all my teeth fell out one after the other. What does that mean?"

The dream reader listened attentively and thought.

"My Imperial Highness," he finally replied, "I'm afraid I have to tell you some bad news. Your teeth in the dream symbolize your relatives and friends. You will lose them all one by one – just as you lost your teeth in the dream."

The emperor became very angry and had the dream reader locked up in the dungeon.

He ordered another dream reader to come to him. He also told him about the dream and asked him what meaning he recognized.

"My Imperial Highness," replied the dream reader, "I am happy to give you a joyful announcement. You will be older than all your relatives and friends. You will outlive them all."

The emperor liked the interpretation and richly rewarded the dream reader handsomely.

The Lucky Guy

A young man had many great plans for the future. However, he felt that he simply had little luck in life, which prevented him from achieving his goals. He decided to visit a wise hermit who lived in a hut in the forest.

So he set off into the forest. At the beginning of his journey, he met a wolf. "Where are you going, young man?" asked the wolf.

"I'm going to the hermit so that he can make a lucky guy out of me."

"When you meet him, can you ask him why I'm always so hungry?"

The young man promised the wolf to ask the hermit this question and went on his way.

Shortly after, he met a young woman sitting by a lake, very distressed. When the woman saw the young man, she asked him where he was going.

"I'm going to the hermit, so that he can make a lucky guy out of," the young man replied.

"When you meet him, be kind enough to ask him why I'm always so sad."

The young man promised to do so and went on his way. A little later, after he had almost circled the lake, he met a willow on the lakeshore, which also inquired where he was going.

The young man answered again that he was going to the hermit in order to be made into a lucky guy.

"When you meet him," said the willow, "please ask him why I am always so thirsty, even though I am standing here by the water."

The young man also promised this and continued his journey. Finally, he reached the hermit's hut and went inside:

"I came because I've always had bad luck in life so far. Don't you think that's unfair and I should be lucky for a change? Please make me a lucky guy."

The hermit nodded and affirmed this.

The young man thanked him and asked the questions of the wolf, the young woman and the willow. After the hermit had answered all the questions, the young man hurried back home so as not to miss anything. After all, he was now a lucky guy.

He almost ran past the tree out of excitement, but it called out to him.

"Did you meet the hermit? Did he answer my question?"

"Yes," the young man replied as he passed, "he said that your roots don't get so much water because there is a great treasure buried between your roots and the water. But excuse me, I'm a lucky guy now and I'm in a hurry."

So he hurried on. When he also almost overlooked the young woman, she called out to him, "Young man, have you met the hermit and asked him my question?"

The young man did not even stop but called out to her as he walked by. "Yes, he said that you are unhappy because you are lonely. He said that a young man will come along in a moment. You will fall in love and be happy together for the rest of your lives. But if you'll excuse me, I have to go on. After all, I'm a lucky guy now."

Exhausted from all the walking, he finally met the wolf. He also asked him, "Did you meet the hermit and ask him my question?"

"Yes, I did," the young man replied. "He said I should tell you that you are so hungry because you don't have enough to eat. He also said to tell you that when the fool has come far enough to tell you that, you can eat him."

Hypochondriac

A man was walking down the street with a limp. He dragged his left foot across the asphalt and avoided putting weight on it as much as possible. A passerby saw this and addressed him.

"What happened to your foot?" she asked the man. "Why are you limping?"

"Nothing happened to my foot. It's perfectly healthy, but I'm afraid that a piece of furniture will fall on it tomorrow when I'm moving house and I want to get used to the injury already."

The Cracked Bucket

A woman in Africa had two large buckets. They hung from a pole that she carried across her neck. While one bucket was perfect, the other had a crack. Every day the woman went to the river, filled both buckets with water, and then carried them to her garden. After the long walk, the perfect bucket was still full of water, while the one with the crack lost almost half of the water on the way home. So it happened day after day, week after week, month after month. Again and again, the woman returned home with one full and one half-full bucket.

The perfect bucket was proud of the fact that it brought home all the water and did not lose a drop along the way. The bucket with the crack, on the other hand, blamed itself and felt ashamed that it only did half the job.

Finally, the cracked bucket spoke to the woman.

"I am ashamed and want to apologize to you. The crack makes it impossible for me to bring all the water to your home."

"You have nothing to be ashamed of," the woman replied. "Haven't you noticed that there are beautiful flowers on your side of the path, while there are none on the other side? I have known about the crack for a long time. That's why I sowed flower seeds on your side of the road. Every day on the way home you water the seeds. And for a year I have been able to pick these flowers and decorate my house with them. Without your crack, I would have to do without the flowers that make my house look so beautiful. I am grateful to you for that."

How Poor People Live

A wealthy man from the city took his son to a rural area. He wanted to show him how poor people live. Father and son arrived early in the morning and spent the whole day and night there before leaving the next morning. On the way back, the father started a conversation with his son.

"Did you enjoy our short trip, son?"

"Yes," the son replied, "I found it very interesting."

"And did you see how poor people can be?"

"Oh yes, Father, I saw that."

"So what did you learn from the short stay?"

"I learned that we have one dog, while the people on the farm have four," the son began to tell. "We have a swimming pool that goes to the middle of our yard, while they have a lake that is much bigger. We have magnificent lamps in our garden while they have the stars of the Milky Way. Our terrace reaches the front yard, while they have the whole horizon"

The father was speechless. Such a perspective had not occurred to him.

"Thank you, Father, for showing me how poor we are."

The Smuggler

A smuggler frequently crossed the border from Egypt to Sudan. He always took different border crossings. Sometimes he went with one camel, sometimes with two or even with three camels. The camels were loaded with hay. The border guards knew that he was a known smuggler. They searched him very carefully each time. They poked the hay bales with pointed sticks, and now and then they even burned some of the hay and searched the ashes for whatever he was smuggling. But not once did they find anything. The smuggler, however, became more prosperous as the years went by. When the smuggler had amassed enough wealth, he retired. One day, one of the former border guards met him.

"Many years have passed, and your smuggling deeds are no longer punishable," said the former border guard. "Now can you please tell me what were you smuggling all those years?"

The smuggler smiled and replied, "Camels!"

This Certainly Has Its Good!

One count had a servant who, on every occasion, however appropriate or inappropriate, was wont to say, "This certainly has its good!" He spoke this sentence so often that it got on the count's nerves.

One day, the count was hunting with his servant. The hunt was also a success because the count had already shot a deer at the beginning. Shortly after, he had also finished off a hare. The two decided to eat the hare on the spot. The servant took care of the campfire while the count prepared the hare. In the process, he clumsily cut off almost his entire little finger.

His faithful servant had nothing better to say about it than, "This certainly has its good!"

The count lost his composure. "What's good about it?" He dismissed his servant and ordered him to leave immediately.

When the count was about to eat the hare, he was attacked by wild barbarians from a nearby village. They were happy to be able to sacrifice a count to their gods soon. At the last moment, a barbarian noticed the missing finger. This meant to the barbarians that the count was imperfect and could not be sacrificed. According to the customs of the barbarians, only unscathed bodies could be sacrificed to the gods. Thereupon the barbarians released the count and he hurriedly went back to his castle. On the way home, he remembered the words of his footman: *This certainly has its good!*

When he arrived at the castle, he immediately sent for his servant and told him what had happened to him in the forest.

"It's good what happened to my finger. It saved my life after all. But it wasn't right of me to dismiss you and send you away. I want you back in my service."

"My count," the servant took the floor, "if you hadn't sent me away, the barbarians would certainly have sacrificed me to their gods. For my body is unharmed. By releasing me, you have saved my life."

The Guilty River

A greengrocer had not been able to sell all his wares and was now riding home on a donkey with the remaining stock. As every day, he had to cross a river, but because the seller had crossed the river many times before he knew where the river was not deep and where there were appropriate stones to step on. He got off the donkey and they both started to cross the river.

This time, however, his mind was elsewhere. He was annoyed that he had sold so few vegetables earlier and that the rest would not be quite so fresh tomorrow so that he would have to offer them more cheaply. Completely distracted by his thoughts, he stepped on a spot where there was no stone and fell into the river up to his waist. He became even angrier. He insulted the people who had not bought his vegetables, he insulted his donkey's short legs, and he insulted the river.

Finally, he blamed the river for his bad day. He grabbed a branch that was floating by and hit the river with it. As he did so, he shouted out his rage and only got wetter. The donkey had gone straight across the river and watched as the greengrocer beat the river with a branch.

After a while, the donkey was dry again. The merchant was still standing in the river, cooled down with time from the cold water, and got a runny nose.

Finally, however, the greengrocer also crossed the river, sat on the donkey, and headed home. As he did so, he explained to the donkey exactly how he had just punished the river.

"That stupid river wanted to annoy me. It is its fault that I have a cold now. But I really showed him."

The Long Rope

The Sultan gathered his advisors and then laid out a rope on the ground.

"You must neither cut nor knot this rope, but I want you to shorten it anyway," he urged his advisors.

All the advisors pondered and discussed it for a while about how the rope could be shortened without cutting it or knotting.

Then one advisor stood up, took a longer rope, and laid it out on the ground next to the Sultan's rope.

A Good Man at the Gates of Hell

Hell was already crowded and there was still a line in front of the entrance. The Devil himself went to the entrance to determine who should take the last place in Hell.

"I have only one spot left," he announced to the crowd. "This I will give to the greatest sinner amongst you."

He questioned the people one by one about their sins. But there was no one who had led such a strongly sinful life. It took a while for the Devil to question everyone. Then, he suddenly noticed an inconspicuous man whom he had over-looked.

"What did you do on Earth to end up here?" he asked the man.

"Nothing. I'm a good man and only here by accident."

"But you must have done something," the Devil persisted. "Everyone sins at some time in his life."

"I have never sinned," the man insisted. "But I have observed many other people sin. I have seen people starve children to death, sell people into slavery, make the poor do hard labor for them, and even force children to work. All around me, people have benefited from evil of every kind. I alone resisted temptation and did nothing."

The Devil listened attentively, before asking. "You witnessed all of this and did nothing?"

"Yes," the man replied, "it all happened practically in front of my porch."

"And you did nothing?"

"Yes!" the man answered very firmly. "I did nothing!"

"Congratulations! Come on in, the last spot is yours."

A Bad Request

At the *Battle of the Three Emperors,* Emperor Napoleon Bonaparte was riding along one of the ramparts when an enemy artillery shell was aimed at him. A French soldier noticed this and started shouting, causing Napoleon's horse to stop short and the artillery shell to miss Napoleon.

"Your ingenuity saved me," Napoleon said to the soldier. "For this I will reward you. Tell me, what do you wish for?"

"Our commander treats me very badly. I want to be assigned to another commander."

"You fool! Become a commander yourself!"

Lao Tzu and the Useless Tree

Lao Tzu and his students were walking through the forest when they came to a place where lumberjacks were cutting down trees. Together they watched the lumberjacks, who had already cut down all but one of the trees. The remaining tree was large and had an enormous number of branches. Hundreds of people could stand under its shade.

Lao Tzu told one of his students to ask the lumberjacks why this particular stately tree was not cut down. The student went to the lumberjacks and asked them the question.

"This tree is completely useless," one of the lumberjacks answered him. "It has too many gristles and branch forks. It cannot be used to make decent boards for carpenters in woodworking. Even for firewood the tree is unsuitable, because its wood makes an unpleasant smoke when burnt. The smoke not only smells bad, but it can also severely affect eyesight if it comes into contact with the eyes. Therefore, we have no use for this tree at all."

The student thanked the lumberjack for the detailed answer and passed it on to Lao Tzu. He then began to grin.

"Be completely useless like this tree," Lao Tzu spoke to his students. "If you are useful, you will be cut up and made into furniture in someone else's house. If you are beautiful, you will be made into merchandise and sold in the marketplace." He raised a finger admonishingly before continuing. "Be like this tree, completely useless. Then you will be able to grow in peace, grow old, and hundreds will find shade under you."

The Decision to Save the World

One woman made an important decision: since the Earth was full of sorrow and hardship, she wanted to start improving the whole world the very next day.

When she got up the next morning, the planned undertaking seemed a bit too ambitious. She first decided to free the country in which she lived from sorrow and hardship. But after only a few weeks, however, did she admit to herself that even this was too difficult an undertaking.

She focused her attention on the city where she lived. But she did not succeed in encouraging the city dwellers to be more virtuous. The same was the case for the district and street where she lived.

When the good woman finally realized that she would probably not even succeed in getting her own family to be more virtuous, she made the decision that she must first and foremost start with herself.

Two Apples

A girl was swinging in the garden when her younger sister arrived with two apples in her hands.

"Will you give me an apple?" the older sister asked the younger. "I want to eat it."

The younger sister thought for a moment. Then she bit into one apple, then the other. The older sister was visibly disappointed and did not hide it.

But only a short moment passed before the younger sister handed her one of the apples.

"Here, sis," she said. "Take this one, it's sweeter."

The Book

During a lecture in a packed hall, the professor held up a book.

"This book is black," he noted.

But all the students saw that the book was obviously red. "No," they shouted, "that book is red."

But the professor persisted and repeated his statement, "Yes, this book is black!"

"That's wrong!" exclaimed the students. "It's red!"

The professor then turned the book over and, lo and behold, the back of the book was black.

It became quiet in the lecture hall until the professor began to speak.

"Never tell anyone they are wrong until you have looked at things from their perspective."

Cleverly Asked

In a very small monastery were two monks. Both were heavy chain smokers who smoked even during prayer. They felt guilty about their habit, so each of them wrote a letter to the bishop to ask his opinion.

After a few days, they received a reply. To their astonishment, permission to smoke was granted to one monk, but denied to the other.

The monk who was allowed to smoke asked, "What did you ask the bishop?"

The monk who had been denied permission replied, "I asked if I could smoke while praying. And you?"

"I asked if I could pray while smoking."

Answers from God

In a dream, a man met God on Mount Sinai, just as Moses did several thousand years ago.

Excited, he asked God the first question that came to his mind. "What surprises you most about humans?"

"Many things!" replied God. "It surprises me that they think so much about the future that they completely forget about the present. As children, people want to grow up as quickly as possible. As adults, they long to be children again. They live as if they would never die, and they die as if they had never lived. They neglect their health to make a lot of money, and then spend a lot of money to get well again."

The man became quite thoughtful before asking the next question. "What lessons should humans learn for life?"

God answered with a smile. "They should learn that deep wounds can be inflicted on a person in seconds, but take a long time to heal. A rich person is not the one who has the most; rather, a rich person is the one who needs the least. The most precious thing is not material wealth, it is the people in one's life. Love cannot be forced. It is not good to compare oneself with others: Everyone is measured according to his abilities and deeds. One can learn to forgive by practicing forgiveness. Some people love deeply but do not know how to express their love. A true friend is someone who knows everything about you and loves you anyway. And that two people can look at the same thing and see completely different things."

The man listened intently and still had many questions. But, unexpectedly, he was torn out of his dream by his little daughter, who woke him up. As he hugged her, he smiled and thought of the dream he had just experienced.

VI
ACCEPTANCE

Trees do not deny their shade to anyone,
not even the lumberjack.

– Hindu wisdom

The King Cobra

A king cobra settled near a village. With her considerable size and aggressiveness, she terrified the villagers.

Every morning the snake was on the main road at the entrance of the village. The villagers had to take long detours to avoid contact with the snake.

One day, a swami came along the main road to the village and approached the king cobra. He showed no fear of the snake. When the king cobra saw the swami approaching, she sprang up, stretched her head, and began to hiss. To her surprise, the swami was not frightened. Instead, he looked at the snake kindly and lovingly, as if she were a good old friend of his. The cobra had not experienced anything like this before. The swami's look did so much good that her anger instantly vanished.

The swami looked at her kindly and spoke in a gentle voice: "Look, now you are no longer aggressive and fearful, but cheerful and joyful. If you are aggressive toward other living beings, you are not doing yourself any good. I have been living for many years according to the motto of not having bad thoughts, not saying anything bad, and not harming anyone. Thus I live in complete harmony with myself and my environment. And as you can easily see, I am happy."

These words made the king cobra think. She realized that her life so far had been characterized by anger, aggression and violence. That's why she was always irritated and dissatisfied. But at that moment everything was completely different: she was calm, relaxed and cheerful. She decided to change. The snake thanked the swami for this lesson and promised him that from now on she would treat all living beings with goodwill and love.

Days passed, and the changed behavior of the king cobra gradually caught the attention of the villagers. She no longer met the villagers with aggression but basked calmly in the sunny spots of the village.

The villagers' fear of the snake diminished, and they decided to take revenge. One villager started attacking the snake with a stick and inflicted some injuries on her. Others threw stones at her and hurled her around. The days passed and the abuse continued. The snake did not understand what was happening. She began to doubt whether her change in outlook had been the right decision.

The swami returned to check on the king cobra and was worried when he saw her: she was emaciated, lying powerless on the grass, and had numerous wounds. "How are you?" he asked anxiously. "What has happened to you?"

"Actually, I'm fine," the snake replied. "Sure, I've lost weight because I don't eat mice anymore. I now feed only on dead animals or forest fruits."

"But you are covered with wounds. Who did this to you?"

"When the villagers realized that I had changed, they gradually lost their fear and began to mistreat me. In the end, even the children tortured me for fun. And so I'm pondering whether your advice is always applicable."

The swami was visibly irritated: "Yes, I advised you not to harm any living being, and to instead treat them with goodwill and love. But I did not say that you should put up with everything if someone wants to do you harm. In such cases, as a defensive reaction, you can leap up and hiss to drive away the offenders. By doing so, you do not inflict physical harm on the attacker, but show that you wish to remain unmolested."

The words made perfect sense to the snake. She wondered why she hadn't thought of it herself.

Learn from the Earth!

When Rahula was mature enough to hear and understand certain teachings, his father said to him: "Rahula, learn from the soil! Whether people cover it with pretty flowers, pour perfume or fresh milk on it, pour stinking excrement, urine, or blood on it, or even spit on it, the soil receives everything equally. Learn from the water! When people wash dirty things in it, the water is not angry or sad. Learn from the fire! Fire burns all things without distinction. It is not ashamed to burn impure substances. Learn from the air! The air carries all odors, be they fragrant or fetid."

Three Floating Robes

Three advanced monks went to the beach every day to bathe. They were so wise and virtuous that minor miracles happened to them every day. For example, it was common that when they took off their robes for bathing, they were carried in the air by the wind. All the time the monks were bathing in the sea, their robes were floating in the air.

One day the monks were bathing in the sea and saw a seagull catch a fish and fly away with it in its mouth.

Then one of the monks said, "Bad seagull!" and immediately his robe fell to the ground.

Then the second monk said, "Poor fish." His robe also abruptly fell to the ground and remained on the sand.

The third monk watched as the seagull flew away with the fish in its mouth. The bird flew on and on until it was no longer visible. All this time the monk remained silent and his robe floated in the air.

Human Nature

A concerned citizen came to a fakir. "Can you please help me?" he asked. "I am at my wit's end. I'm finding it harder and harder to control my growing anger."

"Tell me," the fakir prompted the citizen, "what's bothering you?"

"It's just the way my fellow humans are. They constantly criticize everything and everyone but they are blind to their own faults. I don't want to criticize them either, because then I would just act like them. But it makes me angry to see them doing it all the time."

"I see. Didn't you narrowly escape death a month ago?"

"Yes, I almost died. I was picking mushrooms in the forest and was surprised by a pack of wolves. I immediately climbed the nearest tree. Without water and food, I struggled to survive for two days."

The fakir listened to him attentively and asked how he had escaped the hopeless situation.

"I always waited for the perfect opportunity when the wolves were careless for a moment," replied the man. "Then I climbed down, ran to the next tree, and climbed up. In this way, I moved from tree to tree, closer and closer to the village, until a hunter heard me scream and drove the wolves away."

"During those two days, were you angry at the wolves even once?"

"No, why should I have been? That thought never crossed my mind."

"But the wolves wanted to kill you."

"Yes, but that's what wolves do: they go hunting, look for prey, kill it, and feed on it. That's in their nature, they can't help it."

The fakir smiled and said, "Right as rain! Keep that thought in mind, as it applies to your problem: criticizing others and not noticing your own faults is something a lot of people do. It's something we all do from time to time. It's human nature. So the next time you see people behaving this way, try to accept it and not let anger arise. Of course, you should protect yourself from such behavior and keep a certain distance, but the most important thing is not to feel offended or attacked by it because people are just being themselves. It's in their nature to criticize and judge, so it would be absurd to take offense."

Hakuin and the Child

Zen master Hakuin lived in a village and was highly respected by the villagers. They all wanted to be taught spiritually by him.

One day, the daughter of a villager became pregnant. The father was stunned because his daughter was unwed. He desperately wanted his daughter to tell him the name of the father-to-be. Finally, to avoid the father's punishment, she simply said the name Hakuin. The father, full of indignation, ran to Hakuin, reproached him, and indignantly told him that his daughter had confessed to him that he was the father of the child.

All Hakuin said in reply was, "Is that so?"

The scandal spread like wildfire through the village and beyond. Hakuin lost his good reputation, but this did not bother him. No one sought him out anymore. But even that did not affect him.

When the child was born, the father brought it to him. "You are the father, so take care of the child," he said to the Zen master.

And Hakuin did. He lovingly took care of the child. Everywhere he went, he took the child with him. Whether it rained or stormed, he went out to beg for food and milk for the infant. Many of his once loyal disciples turned away from him. They thought it was a disgrace that Hakuin should have impregnated the young girl. But Hakuin did not utter a single word about it and treated the child as his own.

At some point, the mother could no longer bear the pain of being separated from her child and confessed to her father the real name of the boy with whom she had fathered the child. It was a simple boy from the village and not Hakuin. The girl's father then hurried to Hakuin, prostrated himself before him, and begged his forgiveness.

Hakuin only replied, "Is that so?" and returned the child.

VII
THANKFULNESS

If "thank you" were the only prayer you ever say,
it would be enough.

– Meister Eckhart

A Hermit's Journey

One day, an enlightened hermit went on a journey through the country and met a man without arms and legs, who could hardly move.

"Who are you?" the man asked him.

"I am the enlightenment," replied the hermit.

"If you are the enlightenment, can you heal me?"

"I will heal you, but you will soon forget me and your disability."

The man was baffled by the hermit's words. "How could I ever forget you?" he asked.

"All right," the hermit finally agreed, "I'll come back in seven years, then we'll see if you've forgotten me."

He put his hand on the man's head, who then immediately had arms and legs again.

The hermit moved on and met a homeless man.

"Who are you?" asked the homeless man.

When the hermit told him that he was the enlightenment, the homeless man asked if he could get him somewhere to live.

"I could," said the hermit, "but you will soon forget me and your problem."

"How could I ever forget you?"

Again the hermit agreed. "Well, I'll come back in seven years and we'll see if you have forgotten me."

He put his hand on the head of the homeless man. No sooner had this happened than the homeless man had a house to live in.

The hermit continued his journey. He met a blind man who also asked him who he was.

"I am the enlightenment," replied the hermit.

"The enlightenment?" the blind man asked in amazement. "Can you give me back my sight?"

"Yes, I could, but you will soon forget me and your blindness."

"How could I ever forget you?"

The hermit finally agreed even to the blind man. "All right, I'll come back in seven years, then we'll see if you've forgotten me."

He put his hand on the blind man's head and immediately restored the man's sight.

Seven years then passed and the hermit set out again on a journey to meet the people he had helped long ago. He transformed himself into a blind man and went first to the man to whom he had restored sight.

"Help me," he begged the formerly blind man, "I can't see anything and I urgently need some water."

"How dare you?" the man retorted. "I don't let handicapped people drink my water!"

Immediately the hermit revealed himself. "You see! Seven years ago you were blind. I cured you then, and you promised never to forget your blindness and me."

He put his hand on the ungrateful man's head, who then became blind again.

The hermit continued his journey and met the man to whom he had given arms and legs seven years ago. He made his own limbs vanish and again asked for water.

"Get away!" the man shouted.

The hermit revealed himself. "You see! Seven years ago I cured you of your disability. At that time you promised never to forget me and your disability."

Thereupon he put his hand on the head of the ungrateful man, who immediately lost his arms and legs again.

Finally, the hermit went to the man for whom he had created a house seven years ago. He transformed himself into a homeless man and asked, "May I sleep with you for one night?"

"Gladly, come on in, have a seat, poor thing. I used to be homeless too. It was just seven years ago when the enlightened hermit came and helped me out of homelessness. At that time he said that he would come back after seven years. Wait here until he comes. Maybe he will help you too."

No sooner had the man finished speaking that the hermit revealed himself. "I am the enlightened hermit. You are the only one of the people I helped at that time who has not forgotten me. Therefore, you shall keep your house and always remain happy." In farewell, the hermit added, "We live in constant change. Happiness often turns into misfortune. Adversity turns into wealth and love can turn into hate. No human should ever forget that."

Two Best Friends

Two best friends decided to go hiking in the Sahara. They had been walking for several hours and were very exhausted. An impassioned argument ensued and one of them, in the heat of the moment, punched the other in the face. The beaten man was offended. Without responding, he knelt down quietly and wrote the following words in the sand: *Today my best friend hit me in the face.*

They continued their hike and shortly after arrived at an oasis. There, they wanted to take a break and bathe. The friend who had been hit before suddenly got stuck in the mud and could not free himself. He was in danger of drowning. With great difficulty, his best friend rescued him.

After the rescued friend washed the mud off him, he took a stone and carved the following words into it: *Today my best friend saved my life.*

The other friend watched him curiously. "When I offended you, you wrote your sentence in the sand," he began when the other had finished. "Why do you carve the words on a stone now and not in the sand again?"

"If someone offends or insults us," his friend replied, "we should write it in the sand so the wind can blow it away. But if someone does something good to us, it should be engraved on a stone so that no wind can ever blow it away."

In the Hammam

Nasrudin liked to visit the Turkish bathhouse to bathe and relax. One day, there were new bath attendants working in the hammam who did not know him. He was surprised to not even be greeted by them. After all, it was customary for each bather to receive a soap and two towels. Nasrudin not only received no soap but was also given two old towels with holes in them. Throughout his visit, the bath attendants served Nasrudin very unkindly. When he was finished, he gave them a proud tip and made his way home in a huff.

The bath attendants were surprised at the large tip and regretted being so rude to Nasrudin. They thought that if they had treated Nasrudin better, they would have received an even higher tip.

After a week, Nasrudin came to the hammam again. The bath attendants were as if they had been exchanged: they gave him plenty of soap and new towels. They took turns outdoing each other in their courtesies. Nasrudin was treated like a sultan and enjoyed his stay very much. When he left, he gave each bath attendant a very paltry tip. They looked at Nasrudin in amazement.

Then he said, "Today's tip is for last week's treatment. Last week's tip was for today's treatment."

The Marbles

An old woman never left the house without first putting a handful of marbles in her left pocket. She always took the marbles with her to more consciously perceive and appreciate the most beautiful moments of the day. This way she kept the moments better in her memory.

Be it a pleasant conversation on the street, the laughter of a child, a delicious meal, a shady place on a bench in the park, the radiance of the sun, time in nature – for each such and similar positive experiences, she took a marble from her left pocket and placed it in her right.

In the evening, she would sit on her porch and count the marbles from her right pocket. In so doing, she mentally relived the pleasant moments and was grateful for all she was able to experience.

Matters of Course

A father was sitting on the train with his teenage son. The son was thrilled. With his eyes wide open, he looked out the window.

"Dad, is that a horse?" he asked his father.

The father smiled. "Yes, that is a horse," he answered his son.

"Dad, that tree there is an oak tree, isn't it?"

"Yes, that's an oak tree."

Many more questions followed as the train rolled along the tracks. "Dad, is that a plane? Dad, is there snow? Dad, is that a lake?"

The father patiently affirmed everything and showed his son more sights on his own. "Look, son, that's a mallard duck in the lake over there. And that tree there is a weeping willow. Right next to it is a tent set up with a barbecue area."

A passenger observed the two. "With all due respect," he finally began, "your son's behavior is odd. For such cases there is surely medical or psychological help to which you can turn."

"You're absolutely right!" the father responded. "We have just come from such a specialized clinic. My son lost his sight at the age of six and has only been able to see again since yesterday."

The man looked down at first, embarrassed, and then turned to the young man. "Young man, my apologies to you."

The son accepted the apology.

After a short pause, the passenger added, "And I want to thank you both. This has made me realize how self-evident such little things are to me, and that I don't value them enough. If I lost my eyesight, I would surely miss it a lot."

VIII

RIVALRY

To see the universal and all-pervading
Spirit of Truth face to face,
one must be able to love the meanest of creation as oneself.

– Mahatma Gandhi

The Mysterious Beggar Bowl

An aristocrat was walking through the city with his servant and met a beggar.

"If you want to give me something, then it must be on my terms," the beggar said.

The aristocrat, who had absolutely no intention of donating anything to the beggar, was completely blown away by the statement and became very curious.

"What am I hearing? A beggar who lives on alms and sets conditions for them? Fine, what are your terms?"

"I will accept your alms only if you succeed in filling my beggar's bowl to the brim."

The aristocrat felt provoked by the beggar. After all, he was the richest city dweller. "What makes you think I can't fill your dirty little beggar's bowl? I'm not a beggar like you!" Confident of victory, he decided to fill the bowl. What he didn't know, however, was that the beggar was a yogi and his beggar's bowl was no ordinary bowl.

The aristocrat ordered his servant to fill the beggar's bowl. But when he put copper and silver coins into the bowl, something mysterious happened: the coins disappeared as fast as the servant threw them in.

When the aristocrat saw this, he ordered his servant, "Go on, don't stop!"

The servant threw all the silver and even some gold coins into the bowl. But all the coins disappeared immediately. The aristocrat became more and more furious – at no price in the world did he want to give in and provide the beggar a triumph. He ordered his servant to fetch more gold and precious stones from his residence. The servant did as he was told. When he hurried back from the residence, he threw everything one by one into the bowl. But, as before, everything simply dissolved into thin air. The whole spectacle went on until the aristocrat had lost his entire fortune to the beggar's bowl.

Finally, the aristocrat came to his senses. "I have offended you," he said to the beggar. "I ask you to forgive me. Can you tell me the secret of your beggar's bowl? How is it that all my treasures have disappeared in it?"

The beggar smiled at him. "I made the bowl out of the same matter that the human ego is made of," he replied. "The ego can never get enough. No matter what you give it, it is never satisfied."

Three Monks

Three monks were meditating by a river.

Suddenly, one monk stood up. "I forgot my mat," he said.

He crossed the river, walking over the water. On the other side of the river was their hut. He took the mat and again crossed the river back to the other two monks and continued meditating.

After a few minutes, the second monk stirred. "Ah, I have to do my laundry." He, too, walked over the water of the river to complete his task on the other side. He then returned across the river in the same manner and continued his meditation.

The third monk observed how the two monks crossed the river without any effort. He assumed it was a test of his own abilities. "So you think your abilities are superior to mine?" he said challengingly. "Then watch!"

He walked quickly to the edge of the river. But no sooner did he set his foot on the water, he fell into waist-deep water. He tried again and again, but he did not succeed in keeping himself above the water.

The other two monks watched him do this. Then one asked the other, "Do you think we should tell him where the stepping stones are?"

The Wind and the Sun

The wind and the sun argued about which of the two would manage to get the hiker to take off his jacket faster.

The wind tried first and blew as hard as it could. But the hiker did just the opposite of what the wind intended: he buttoned up his jacket. The wind raged and stormed for all it was worth. But the hiker pulled his jacket tighter and tighter to withstand the wind. After a while, the wind gave up.

Then it was the sun's turn. It sent its warm rays of sunshine to the hiker. Without wind and with the warmth of the sun, the hiker felt pleasantly warm and unbuttoned his jacket. It was not long before he took off his jacket.

Three Sons

Three women went to the river in the morning to draw water for the day. They each had a son.

The first woman began to praise her son. "You should hear my son sing. He has the voice of an angel."

The second woman joined in. "My son is incredibly strong for his age. He can throw stones very far."

But the third woman remained silent. The first two women took this to mean that her son was not particularly good at anything.

After all three had filled their buckets, they set off again on their way home. Halfway home, their three sons happened to meet them. The first son sang as beautifully as an angel, while the second threw stones around. The third, however, ran to his mother to take the heavy bucket from her.

An old man was sitting on a bench watching this.

"Well, old man?" asked the first woman. "What do you say to our three sons?"

"Three sons?" the man wondered. "I see only one."

IX
OPINIONS

Turn your face to the sun,
and the shadows will fall behind you.

– African wisdom

The True Value of the Ring

A lad asked a wise man for advice.

"People tell me I'm good for nothing," he said. "They say I'm stupid and that whatever I do I do wrong. Meanwhile, I feel useless and I'm not motivated to do anything. What can I do to make people have a higher opinion of me?"

"I'm sorry, but I can't help you now," the sage replied. "I have a problem of my own that I need to take care of first." After a short pause, he continued, "But you could help me with my problem first, so it would be solved faster and I could take care of your problem afterward."

The lad was surprised that the sage asked him for assistance. "I would like to help you. What do you want me to do?"

The sage pulled a ring from his little finger and handed it to the fellow. "Take my horse and ride to the marketplace. I have debts and am forced to sell this ring. I ask you to negotiate the best possible price. Do not sell it for less than one gold coin."

The lad jumped on the horse and hurried to the marketplace. Once there, he offered the ring of the sage to the merchants. Almost all of them were interested in it. However, when he demanded a gold coin for it, he was laughed at. No one was willing to pay such a high price for it. An old seller politely said to him, "The ring is beautiful and valuable, but a gold coin is too high a price for it."

After presenting the ring to all the buyers, three silver coins was the best offer he received. Disappointed that he could not sell the ring, he got on the horse and rode back to the sage. On the ride, doubts plagued him. After all, he wanted to sell the ring at a good price and help the sage with his problem.

"I'm sorry," the lad reported when he arrived at the sage's house. "I could have gotten at most three silver coins for it. I didn't manage to convince anyone of the true value of the ring."

The sage smiled and said, "What you say is very important. Indeed, we must first determine its true value. Please ride again to the center of the city, but this time to a jewelry merchant, not to the marketplace. He can best determine how much the ring costs. Tell him that you want to sell the ring and he should give you his highest bid. But whatever he will offer you for it, you must not sell the ring under any circumstances. Return it to me."

Once again, the lad went to the city. The jewelry merchant examined the ring very thoroughly and said, "Tell the sage that if he sells his ring now, I will give him thirty-six gold coins for it."

"Thirty-six gold coins?!" exclaimed the fellow in utter amazement.

"Yes. Actually, the ring is worth more, but I only have thirty-six gold coins available at the moment. Without such haste, the sage could sell the ring for even more."

The lad hurried back to the sage to tell him the good news. The sage listened attentively to everything the lad had to tell him.

"Sit down," said the sage after the fellow had finished. "Do you understand now? You are like this ring: a piece of jewelry, precious and unique. And just like this ring, only an expert in his field can recognize your true value. So why do you let yourself be guided by the opinion of others who don't know you as well as you do?"

While the sage was saying this, he put his ring back on his little finger. Then the lad realized that the sage never intended to sell his ring.

Trying to Please Everyone

A grandfather was on his way to the marketplace with his granddaughter and a donkey. He was sitting on the donkey and his granddaughter was leading the donkey on a leash. A villager observed this.

"Unbelievable!" he shouted angrily. "He just lets the little girl walk next to the donkey. How can anyone sit around so lazily on the donkey while the child is tiring herself out?"

Taking the villager's remark to heart, the grandfather got off the donkey and put his granddaughter on the animal. They continued on their way until the next villager noticed them.

"I don't believe it!" he exclaimed. "The girl sits on the donkey like a queen and the old man has to walk."

Thereupon the grandfather sat down behind his grand-daughter on the donkey. It was not long before another villager made his comment.

"What cruelty to animals!" he shouted across the street. "The poor donkey. How can two people ride such a small donkey?"

Finally, grandfather and granddaughter got down from the donkey and led it by the leash to the marketplace. The next villager saw this.

"You are really too stupid," he said. "You already have a donkey, and yet you just walk alongside it."

The grandfather looked at his granddaughter and said, "No matter what you do, there will always be people who criticize and judge you. Never worry about what others think, but act with love and kindness."

The Favorite Student

It is said that Laith was a favorite student of Junayd. The other students were quite envious of him. This did not escape Junayd's notice. He gathered his students and said, "I notice your envy toward Laith. I will demonstrate to you why he is the most well-behaved and understanding of all of you so that you too can recognize it."

Junayd told his students to bring him thirty birds. When this was done, he said, "Now each of you take a bird and kill it in a place where no one is watching. Afterward, come back to me with the bird!"

The students left, killed the birds, and returned – except Laith, who brought the bird back alive. The students wondered why Laith's bird was still alive.

Junaid asked what was on the tip of everyone's tongue, "Laith, why didn't you kill the bird?"

"I couldn't kill the bird," Laith replied, "because you ordered us to kill it in a place where no one is watching."

Who Knows?

There once lived a farmer and his only son in a small hut. The farmer's only possession was a beautiful horse that was used for farm work. There had been countless prospective buyers who offered high prices for the horse, but the farmer refused them all. The villagers, envious of the horse, said, "Farmer, how lucky you are to own such a beautiful horse."

"Who knows?" was the farmer's only reply.

One day, the horse disappeared without a trace. The farmer and his son tried in vain to find it. The villagers came and said, "Now your horse is gone, what bad luck you have."

The farmer looked at them and said, "Who knows?"

Harvest time was approaching and, without the horse, the farmer and son had to work hard. It was doubtful whether they would manage to collect the whole harvest. A few days passed and, lo and behold, the horse came back to the farmer, bringing another horse with it. The villagers were envious and said, "Farmer, how lucky you are, now you even have two horses."

"Who knows?" the farmer replied again.

The next morning, the farmer's son tried to tame the new horse. It was going well, until suddenly it threw him off so violently that he broke both legs. The villagers said to the farmer, "What bad luck you have. Your son can't walk any-more."

Again the farmer replied, "Who knows?"

The farmer toiled hard to collect the harvest in time with-out the support of his son. Meanwhile, a war broke out. The king needed soldiers, and all the young men in the village who were liable for military service were drafted into the army. Only the son of the old farmer was not called up, be-cause his broken legs made him unfit for war. And again the villagers came and said, "Farmer, how lucky you are that your son was not called up for the war."

The farmer simply replied, "Who knows?"

The Mousetrap

On a farm lived a clever mouse. Despite her small eyes, she had a good overview of what was going on at the farm.

One morning, she discovered a mousetrap that the farmer had set up the night before. Sensing danger, she wanted to warn the other animals. She ran to the chicken first and told her about the mousetrap.

"What do I care about a mousetrap?" the chicken replied. "It may be a problem for you, but not for me!"

The mouse ran on and told the goat about the mousetrap.

"I understand your worries and hope you won't fall into the trap," the goat answered her, "but for me the mousetrap is harmless."

Next, the mouse went to the cow. But the cow also saw no reason for concern.

"Do you really think a mousetrap could hurt me?" the cow asked spitefully.

The mouse had warned all the animals on the farm, but no one paid much attention to her. So she went to her hiding place, where she spent the rest of the day full of sadness and worry.

No sooner had the sun risen than the mouse heard a snap – the mousetrap had shut!

The farmer's wife went into the kitchen to see if the mouse had been trapped. When she turned on the light, she was bitten by a poisonous snake whose tail was caught in the trap. The farmer was awakened by his wife's scream and ran into the kitchen. Immediately, both rushed to the emergency room, where the farmer's wife received medical treatment and thus survived the snake bite.

In order for his wife to recover faster, the farmer decided to cook a chicken broth. For this, he slaughtered the chicken.

When the farmer's wife left the hospital in good health, the neighbors were invited to celebrate. For this special occasion, the goat was slaughtered. A few days passed and the farmer received mail. It was the bill from the hospital, which was much higher than expected. In order to pay the required sum, the farmer was forced to slaughter the cow.

The mouse, who had been watching all this, reflected on the last few days: *Why didn't they all take my warning seriously? Why didn't they understand that a problem that affects one of us can also affect everyone else?*

The Sermon

An imam came to a mosque to give a sermon. However, there was only one man in the hall.

"There is no one here but you," said the imam in amazement. "Do you think I should give the sermon anyway?"

"Listen, I am a simple man," the man began, "I don't know anything about all that. But if I come to a stable and see that all but one horse has run away, I will feed the remaining horse anyway."

The imam then gave his sermon, which lasted for two hours. Afterward, he felt happy and satisfied. He asked the man what he thought of the sermon.

"As I said," the man replied, "I am a simple man and I don't know much about such things. But if I come to a stable and see that all the horses have run away except one, I will still feed it. I wouldn't give it all the feed, though."

The Most Delicious Vegetable in the World

Once Nasrudin became the ruler's closest confidant. The cook had discovered a new recipe with eggplants and prepared the meal for the ruler, as the ruler enjoyed the vegetables very much.

"Isn't this the most delicious vegetable in the whole world?" he asked Nasrudin.

"Yes, Your Majesty, the very best!" replied Nasrudin.

The ruler ordered the cook to serve this dish every day from now on. No sooner said than done. The cook prepared the same dish with eggplants all week long.

On the seventh day, the ruler roared, "I have been eating this dish all week. It no longer tastes good to me. Take away this food immediately!"

Nasrudin again agreed with the ruler. "Yes, Your Majesty, it is the worst vegetable in the whole world!"

The ruler was astonished, "But Nasrudin, just a few days ago you praised this vegetable as the most delicious vegetable. Why the change of mind?"

"Yes, you are absolutely right!" replied Nasrudin. "But after all, I serve the ruler and not the vegetables!"

Recession

A man lived in New York City and owned a hotdog stand. Each day, many customers came and bought his hotdogs. He worked from morning till late in the evening and did not follow the news. The demand for his delicious hotdogs was constantly increasing, and so he decided to open a second stand.

For this undertaking, he had to coordinate with his suppliers and the city government and purchase new equipment. He asked his son who had recently graduated in economics to support him.

The two had almost finished planning when the son came rushing to his father. "Haven't you read it in the newspapers?" he asked his father excitedly. "A severe recession is coming. At such a time, it's fatal to expand because demand and sales will shrink."

The father hadn't heard any of this; after all, day-to-day business was going splendidly. But he thought to himself: *Well, my son has studied, he is always up-to-date with the news and reads the business section every day. After all, he should know what he's talking about.*

Starting from a recession, the man decided to put expansion on hold for the time being. He reduced his sausage and bread order quantities and cut back on food quality. He also reduced his marketing expenditures by placing fewer advertisements. The uncertainty of the impending recession made him increasingly pessimistic, and over time, his customers felt it too.

So it wasn't long before his customer base began to shrink. Soon his once magnificent business was losing money and he was forced to close his only stand. Disappointed, he turned to his son and said, "You were right, son, we are indeed in the midst of a great recession!"

The Three Sieves of Socrates

A woman came hurrying to Socrates, yelling, "Socrates, I have to tell you something!"

"Stop, wait!" interrupted Socrates. "Did you strain what you want to tell me through the three sieves?"

"Three sieves?"

"That's right, three sieves. Let's first see if what you want to tell me fits through the three sieves." Socrates made a gesture with his hand to draw the woman's attention to his words. "The first sieve is the truth," he then began. "Have you checked to make sure that everything you want to tell me is the truth?"

"No, I heard someone tell it and ..."

Socrates interrupted the woman and continued. "All right. But surely you have tested it with the second sieve – the sieve of goodness. If what you want to tell me is not certainly true, is it at least good?"

"No," the woman answered hesitantly, "on the contrary, it is ..."

Again Socrates interrupted. "So let us apply the third sieve. Is it necessary for you to tell me?"

"No, it is not necessary," the woman replied after a moment's thought.

"Well," said Socrates, smiling, "if it is neither true, nor good, nor necessary, you better not tell me nor burden yourself with it."

The Emperor's New Clothes

Hans Christian Andersen once described the story of an emperor who lived many years ago and placed tremendous value on new clothes. This went so far that he spent all his money on them. He had an outfit for every hour of the day.

One day, two impostors came to the emperor's court. They pretended to be weavers and said that they could weave the most beautiful clothes imaginable. Not only would the colors and patterns be unusually beautiful, but the clothes they would sew would possess the property of being invisible to anyone who was stupid or unfit for their profession.

These would be splendid clothes, the emperor thought. *If I had them on, I would immediately recognize which people in my empire are unfit for their profession or stupid. Yes, these clothes must be woven for me at once!*

He commissioned the two supposed weavers. They set up looms in a hall and pretended to weave. They asked for the finest silk and gold and immediately put them in their own pockets. They sat at the empty looms until late at night.

The next morning the emperor wanted to know how far the two weavers had gotten with their work. But he did not dare to ask himself, because the one who was stupid or unfit for his profession would not be able to see what they had made. Therefore, he first sent his minister to the weavers.

The emperor thought, *The minister can best judge how the stuff turns out, because he is clever and absolutely suitable for his profession!*

The minister entered the room where the two impostors were working at the empty looms.

"This can't be true," the minister said to himself, not believing his eyes, "I can't see anything!"

The impostors asked him to come closer and asked if it was not a pretty pattern with beautiful colors. Then they pointed to the empty looms, but the poor minister could see nothing, for there was nothing there.

He thought, *Am I stupid? Surely this can't be. Or am I unfit for my profession? No one must know!*

"Well, you don't say anything about it?" the impostors asked the minister.

"It pleases me very much," the minister replied. "I will immediately report to the emperor."

The impostors demanded more silk and gold, which they said they needed for weaving, but they put it all into their own pockets. They continued to work on the empty looms as before.

The emperor soon sent another statesman to inquire whether his clothes would soon be ready. But the statesman fared as the minister had done before: he could see nothing on the looms.

"Isn't that a pretty piece of clothing?" the two impostors asked him. They showed and explained the magnificent pattern, which was not there at all. Completely irritated and unsettled, the statesman thought to himself, *I am not stupid. Must I therefore be unfit for my profession? No one must know!* And so he praised the clothes, which he did not see, and assured them of his joy at the beautiful colors and splendid pattern. He then reported to the emperor on the progress of the weavers.

Now the emperor wanted to see his clothes for himself while they were still on the looms. With a large entourage, he went to the two impostors, who were weaving with all their might, but without fiber or thread.

"Isn't it magnificent, Your Majesty? This pattern and these colors," said the minister and the statesman, who had been with the weavers before. They pointed to the empty looms, for they thought that everyone else in the room could see the clothes.

The emperor was beside himself and thought: *This is terrible! I can't see anything! Am I stupid? Am I unfit to be emperor? That would be unthinkable!*

Then he answered the weavers. "It's beautiful!" At this, he nodded with satisfaction and looked at the empty looms. He could not admit that he saw nothing. All his companions saw only the empty looms and did the same as the emperor. Everyone praised clothes they could not see.

All night, the impostors were up and had lit extra lights so that people could see that they were very busy finishing weaving the emperor's new clothes. They pretended to take the stuff from the looms, they cut the air with scissors, they sewed with sewing needles without thread, and the next morning they said, "Now the clothes are ready!"

The emperor came and the impostors raised one arm in the air, just as if they were holding something in their hands.

"Look, here are the trousers!" they said in a proud voice. "And here is the shirt! Here is the coat! The pieces are as light as cobwebs. You'd think you had nothing on your body. But that's just the beauty of it, isn't it, Your Majesty?!"

They led the emperor to a large mirror. The emperor took off all his clothes and stood naked before the mirror. The impostors pretended to dress him in the new clothes. When the impostors put on the emperor's last imaginary garment, the emperor said, "Look at my new clothes! Don't they look excellent?" His entourage looked at the naked emperor and complimented him effusively on his new clothes.

Afterward, the emperor walked through the streets to proudly present himself to the people in his new clothes. All the people on the street saw the naked emperor, but no one wanted to admit that they could not see the new clothes, because then they would be considered unfit for their profession or stupid. So all the people said, "What beautiful clothes our emperor is wearing. His new clothes are incomparable."

The emperor continued his walk through the city until suddenly a child cried out, "But he has nothing on!" The comment spread like wildfire until finally, all the people shouted, "But he has nothing on!"

The Important Things in Life

An enlightened woman was on a ship. Next to her sat a scholar who was extremely convinced of himself thanks to his high education.

"Have you ever studied oceanography?" the scholar asked the enlightened woman.

"No," the enlightened one replied.

"Oh, you missed a lot there! Knowledge of currents is indispensable for steering a ship."

They then sat side by side in silence for a while before the scholar asked the next question. "Have you ever studied meteorology?"

"No," the enlightened woman replied to this as well.

"Too bad, you missed a lot there too! If you know about the winds and the weather, you can bring a ship safely and quickly to its destination."

Even after that, the scholar did not let up. "Did you at least study astronomy?"

"No."

The scholar smiled pityingly at the enlightened woman and said, "Too bad you don't have such knowledge. With it, a captain can navigate a ship through all waters."

The woman was silent for a while before asking the scholar, "Have you ever learned to swim?"

"No," he replied, "I simply have not had time for that."

"Too bad, because this ship is sinking right now."

X

GOOD TIMES AND BAD TIMES

When the last tree is cut,
the last fish eaten,
and the last stream poisoned,
you will realize,
that you cannot eat money.

– Wisdom of the Cree

This Too Shall Pass

A king announced to all the scholars and wise men of his kingdom, "I have had the best ring made for me by the best blacksmith. It is made of pure gold, platinum, and diamond. Now I would like you to give me a short message that I can use in any time of need and desperation. The message must be short enough to fit inside of the ring. That way I will always have it with me."

All the great scholars and wise men wrote impressive messages. But they were all far too long to fit inside the ring. None of them could keep it short enough. The king's requirement seemed impossible for them.

Then the king thought of one of his servants, whom he held in high esteem and treated as though he was a member of the family. He said to him, "All the scholars and wise men have failed. Do you have such a message for me?"

"I am not a wise man nor a scholar," replied the old servant. "But I know the message you seek. For there is only one message. Your wise men and scholars cannot give it to you, for it is not written in books. You must have experienced it. As a token of my gratitude for your good treatment of me over all these years in your palace, I give you this message." He wrote a few words on a small piece of paper and folded it up. "Don't read it now," he said to the king as he handed him the piece of paper. "Keep it under your ring, safely tucked away, and don't open it until times of great intensity and stress."

At that moment, the king had no idea that such a time was to come very soon.

The kingdom was attacked and conquered. Alone on horseback, the king tried to flee from the attackers. The enemy forces, who were far superior in numbers, gave chase. He came to a dead end: in front of him was a big wall and around him a very dense forest. If his pursuers met him here, it was guaranteed to be his end. He could already hear the galloping horses coming closer and closer.

Suddenly he remembered the ring and the message it contained. He took out the note and read: *This too shall pass*.

When he read the sentence, he became very calm. This too shall pass...

The horsemen who were pursuing the king took a different path and did not find him. The king then felt great relief and at the same time enormous gratitude toward his servant. He folded up the note again and put it back into the ring.

Some time passed and the king assembled a mercenary force to reconquer his former kingdom. He succeeded in doing so. On the day he returned victoriously to his kingdom, he was celebrated by the crowd. He was very proud of himself.

The old servant walked beside the royal carriage.

"My king, now is also the right time to read the message," said the old servant. "Read it again."

"What do you mean?" the king then asked. "I don't need the message now. I have won, the kingdom is mine again. Can't you see how the people are celebrating me?"

"Listen to me carefully. This message is not only for bad times but also for good times. It doesn't just apply when you're a loser. It's also true when you're a winner. Not only when you are last but also when you are first."

The king took the message out of his ring and read, *This too shall pass*. Suddenly, he was overcome by the same calm, the same silence – in the midst of the cheering crowd. His pride and ego were gone. Everything passes. He asked his servant to take a seat next to him in the carriage.

"I understand now," he said to the servant. "Is there an additional message you want to share with me?"

The old man replied, "Remember that everything passes. Only you remain. You remain eternally as a witness. Everything passes, but you remain. You are the reality. Everything else is just a dream, an illusion, a snapshot. There are beautiful dreams, there are nightmares. But it doesn't matter whether it's a beautiful dream or a nightmare. What matters is who sees the dream. That seeing is the only reality."

A Little Casket

A woman ran a café that sold homemade cakes and treats. For some time, the business was not doing as well as it used to. She was steadily losing customers and sales were plummeting year after year. Full of worry about the development, she turned to a sage who lived not far from town. She told him about her situation and her sorrow.

"My café is moving straight to ruin. Can you please help me?" She turned to the wise man in search of help.

The sage gave the woman a small, locked casket.

"You must carry this casket around with you all day, every day," he instructed her. "In the cellar, in the pantry, in the garden, in every corner of the café – everywhere. It won't do any miracles right away, but after a while, you will feel better. Bring the casket back to me in one year."

The woman was skeptical, but in her desperation, she conscientiously followed the sage's advice. She diligently carried the casket with her. In the process, she discovered many things that she had ceased to notice. First, she began to thoroughly clean the café, pantry, and cellar. She also had the aging chairs and tables restored. She painted the walls and ceilings with fresh paint and redecorated the café. She got a new coffee machine and tried new pastry recipes. She cleared the garden of weeds and planted new beautiful flowers. She put up a rose arch at the entrance and decorated the entire garden so that customers felt comfortable and relaxed enjoying their cup of coffee with a piece of cake.

The year passed and the woman, visibly pleased, went to the sage to return his casket.

"I thank you most sincerely, good man," she said. "Your casket has helped me a lot. My business is flourishing again. I have more customers than ever before. They are happy and come by almost every day. Can you please tell me what this casket is all about? Why was it able to perform the miracle?"

The sage smiled and opened the casket. To her astonishment, the woman saw that the casket was empty.

"The casket was empty all the time," said the sage. "You performed the miracle yourself."

XI
ENVY

It is a royal thing,
when one is doing good
to hear evil spoken of himself.

– Marcus Aurelius

A Tuft of Grass and a Rose

A tuft of grass was deeply sad. The rose, which was right next to it, did not miss it.

"What's wrong with you?" asked the rose. "Why are you letting your blades hang like that?"

"I feel terrible," replied the tuft of grass. "Everyone just tramples on me, but admires you because you are the perfect rose. You are the symbol of romance and love with your beautiful red color. I wish I could be like you."

Suddenly the rose began to cry. "Oh, dear tuft of grass. You can't imagine how much I envy you. I may be beautiful, but I am also unapproachable. People admire me, but if they touch me, I hurt them and they curse and insult me. If only I were like you, so soft and gentle. People, big and small, take off their shoes and socks to feel you. I see how they enjoy being in touch with you. I notice their smiles and pleasure every time."

The tuft of grass had listened carefully to the rose and became thoughtful. It had not considered the situation like this before and realized that all its attention was focused on its disadvantages.

The Donation

A man saw that Rabbi Zusha was very poor. He began to give him ten shekels whenever he went to the prayer house. Weeks passed, and the man noticed that his wealth had been increasing. He found that the more he donated to Zusha, the wealthier he became.

Then the man heard from Rabbi Zusha that he was a disciple of a great ascetic. The man believed that if the donations to the disciple had brought him much prosperity, then the donation to his teacher should bring even more prosperity. So he went to the ascetic, and after much pleading, the man got him to accept a generous donation. But contrary to his expectation, the donor's wealth now began to dwindle.

The man was horrified and, in despair, went back to Zusha.

"When I gave you money, the more I gave, the wealthier I became. But when I gave a large donation to your teacher, it had the opposite effect: my wealth dwindled. Shouldn't the donation to your teacher have resulted in far more wealth?"

"As long as you gave and did not look at whom you gave," Zusha began to explain, "God also gave to you and did not look. But when you began to make calculations and look for choice recipients, God did the same."

Two Sneaky Thieves

A traveler decided to spend the night in an inn.

When he arrived there, the innkeeper welcomed him at the front door. "Take good care of yourself," said the innkeeper. "This village is teeming with thieves. They are so sneaky; they can strip a man's clothes off without him noticing."

"Ah, I'm not worried about that," the traveler replied, "they can't steal from me so easily."

Just at that moment, two thieves stood behind the wall and listened to this conversation.

To be on the safe side, the traveler decided to sleep next to his horse to prevent it from being stolen. But the two thieves were not after his horse, but his clothes. They decided to steal the traveler's clothes even before he fell asleep. They approached him silently.

"Let's hide the treasure here," whispered the one thief to the other.

"Are you out of your mind?" the other thief asked. "Didn't you notice that man over there? If we hide our treasure here, he'll steal it from us, won't he?"

"Yes, of course I noticed him. But he's fast asleep."

"No, he's not asleep."

The thieves argued briefly until the second thief relented. "All right. If you think he's asleep, we'll just undress him. If he's really in a deep sleep, we'll hide our treasure here."

No sooner said than done. They stripped the traveler of all his clothes, even his underwear. Then they dug a hole, filled it with excrement, and covered it again with earth. As soon as the two thieves were out of sight, the now naked traveler rose and began to dig at the same spot. After a short time, as he reached into the excrement with his bare hands, he said to himself, "Yes, my host was right. The thieves here are really sneaky."

The Rich Tourist

A man gained the trust of a rich tourist who was traveling alone in the taiga. Every morning, after getting up, the tourist counted her money. The man was always present, watching her. He made a plan to steal from her.

Throughout the day, the tourist always carried her wallet with her. As soon as she fell asleep, the man searched her suitcases to find the money. He searched under her bed, under her mattress, and even under her pillow. But he could not find the money.

The next morning, the tourist sat there again and counted her money. This was repeated day after day until the man finally approached the woman.

"I'm sorry," he politely began the conversation. "Every night I tried to find your money to steal it. But I didn't succeed. Where do you always hide it?"

The woman began to laugh and replied, "I recognized your intentions early on. That's why I always hid my money under *your* pillow at night. You never looked there!"

Leave Traces

A nobleman knew that he would not be among the living for much longer. He had two sons and was not sure if he had taught them everything important in life.

He said to them, "I am already an old man, the traces and marks I have made in this life will soon fade. I want you to go on a journey to leave your own personal traces and signs. Come back after a year and show me them."

The sons packed their things and set out on the long journey. The elder son began to eagerly carve signs in trees, build stone cairns, and tie grasses together to mark his way. He worked from early morning until late at night. The younger son, on the other hand, focused on the people. He went to the villages, talked to many people, helped them, and celebrated with them. The older brother disliked this. After all, he worked from morning to night, whereas his younger brother mostly enjoyed himself.

The year passed and both sons returned to their father. The three men went to look at the traces left by the two sons. However, not much remained of the traces and signs of the elder son. The rain and wind had caused the cairns to topple over, and the grasses that had been tied before were blown away by the wind. The trees he carved had fallen because of a storm. Wherever they went on their journey, however, children and adults always came to the younger son to play with him or chat. People invited them to eat and celebrate.

After their return, the nobleman spoke to his sons: "You both tried to fulfill my mission of making signs and leaving traces. My elder son, you worked hard and achieved much, but your signs did not last. You, my younger son, left signs and marks in people's hearts. These will remain for a long time."

The King's Garden

A king owned a beautiful garden of which he was very proud. In this garden were many different trees, flowers, and shrubs, including many exotic specimens.

One day, when the king came to his garden, he found the plants withering, so he went to the Douglas fir.

"Douglas fir, please tell me what happened here," he asked.

"I'm dying," the Douglas fir replied, "because I can't grow as tall as the spruce."

The king turned to the spruce, which was drooping its branches because it could not bear grapes like the vine. The vine, in turn, was dying because it could not bloom like the orchids. The king asked the other flowers and shrubs and always got similar answers.

Then he discovered a garden pansy. This one was not wilted like the other flowers, but still blooming and fresh.

"Pansy," asked the king, "why are you so alive, unlike all the other plants here?"

"It was obvious to me that you wanted a pansy when you planted me," the flower replied. "If you had wanted a Douglas fir, a spruce, a vine, or an orchid, you would have planted a Douglas fir, a spruce, a vine, or an orchid. But since you planted me here, I wanted to do my best to comply with your wish. And since I can't be anything else anyway, I'll continue to do my best and be just what I am."

The king was very taken with these words and passed them on to all the plants in his garden.

XII
ENLIGHTENMENT

There exists sorrow.
There is a cause of sorrow.
The sorrow can be eradicated.
There are means for the eradication of sorrow.

– The four noble truths discovered by Buddha Gautama

A Well

A monk went to a well to fetch water for the day. Some villagers saw this and asked him, "Tell us, monk, what meaning do you see in your life of silence and meditation?"

The monk, who was about to draw water from the well, asked the visitors to look into the well. "What do you see?" he asked.

The villagers looked curiously into the deep well and replied, "We see nothing."

After the monk filled his buckets, he asked the villagers to look into the well again.

"Now what do you see?"

The villagers looked down again and then said, "We see ourselves reflected in the water."

"When I had just filled a bucket, the water was restless," the monk explained. "Now the water is calm. This is what we experience in silence and meditation: We see ourselves! And now wait a while."

After a few minutes, the monk asked the villagers to look into the well one more time.

"Now look into the well. What do you see?"

"Now we can even see the stones at the bottom of the well."

The monk then explained, "This is the experience of silence and meditation: if you wait long enough, you will see the cause of all things."

Milarepa

Milarepa is known, among other things, for pressing his hand into a rock in the Himalayas to demonstrate to his disciples that matter is an illusion. The rock has been preserved until today and is regularly visited by pilgrims.

Milarepa had been on a long search for enlightenment. One day he met an old man slowly descending a path with a heavy sack on his shoulder. Intuitively, Milarepa knew that this man knew the secret he had been desperately seeking for so many years.

"Old man," Milarepa addressed him, "tell me, what is enlightenment?"

The old man smiled, silently took the heavy sack from his shoulder, and placed it on the ground.

"Yes, I understand, thank you!" said Milarepa. "But what comes after enlightenment?"

Again the man smiled, bent down, lifted the heavy sack onto his shoulder, and went on his way.

The Mountain

Once upon a time, a man lived near a mountain. Every day he thought about what it would be like to climb the mountain. What would he see at the top?

The day came when he decided to start the journey. At the foot of the mountain, he met a traveler.

"How did you climb the mountain and what did you see from up there?" he asked the traveler.

The traveler told him how he had climbed the mountain and what he saw from up there. The man thought to himself that the way the traveler described to him sounded rather tedious. He decided to look for an easier way.

He continued walking around the foot of the mountain until he met another traveler.

"How did you climb the mountain and what did you see from up there?" he asked this traveler as well.

The traveler answered him. Again, the man thought to himself that the path described also sounded quite arduous. He decided to ask other travelers how they climbed the mountain and what they had seen from the summit. In total, he interviewed twenty travelers. Each traveler took the way that was most suitable for them to climb the mountain. But they all had one thing in common: each way was quite arduous.

The man now knew from all the reports how to climb the mountain and what he would see from the top. He then decided not to climb the mountain and went back to his house.

So he did not even try to climb the mountain and did not see the view for himself.

An Advisor for the King

Once there lived a just king. The welfare of his subjects was close to his heart. His closest confidant and advisor was a wise man. The wise man had also advised the previous king and was now very old. He asked the king to start looking for a successor for his position so that he could train the new advisor while he still lived.

So the king let it be known that he was looking for a successor for his closest advisor. Before long, all those who were distinguished by high education and deep knowledge auditioned in the throne room. The king was not completely satisfied with any of the candidates. Something seemed to be missing in all of them, but the king did not know exactly what it was.

The king told this to the old advisor, who came up with an idea: the king should conduct a selection procedure. Not only sages and scholars should take part in this, but anyone who wanted to.

There was much excitement. After all, almost everyone wanted to be able to advise the king. Each applicant was given a set of one hundred keys. The task was to open a large and heavy door on the first try.

Numerous candidates attempted the challenge and one after the other failed. Days and weeks passed. Suddenly, a traveler appeared in front of the mysterious door. He meticulously examined the lock and the many keys. Without even inserting a key into the keyhole, he grabbed the door handle, pushed it down, and opened the massive door with a little effort.

The king saw this and delightedly said, "You face challenges without being misled. You do not rely on what you hear, but trust your mind and your intuition! You shall be my new advisor!"

The Gift

Once there lived a great warrior who was known throughout the village. He had numerous disciples and, although he was old, he could still defeat any challenger.

A young warrior came to the old master with a firm determination to defeat him. The young warrior was famous for two skills: he was very strong and he also possessed an outstanding ability to recognize and exploit any weakness of his opponent. His strategy was always to wait for his opponent's first blow and then strike him with tremendous power and speed. This is how he had been able to win all his duels so far.

The master accepted the challenge, although his disciples tried to dissuade him. They considered his young challenger to be superior.

The two faced each other ready to fight and the young warrior began to insult the master. He threw dirt at him and even spat in his face. This went on for hours. But the master just stood there, motionless and calm, without throwing the first punch. Finally, the young warrior exhausted himself. He realized that he could not provoke the master to the first blow and accepted his defeat.

The disciples watched all the while, happy on the one hand that their master had won the duel, and disappointed on the other that he had not rebuked the challenger. They asked him, "Master, how could you let yourself be insulted like that?"

The master replied, "If someone comes to you to give you a gift and you do not accept it, whose gift is it?"

Who Are You?

A woman visited Ramana Maharshi. Quietly, she sat down next to him and meditated.

A while passed before Maharshi asked her, "Who are you?"

"I am the mayor's wife," the woman replied.

"I did not ask whose wife you are, but who you are."

"I am the mother of two children."

"I didn't ask you whose mother you are. I asked you who you are."

"I'm a cook."

This answer also did not satisfy Maharshi. "I did not ask about your profession, but who you are."

Somewhat perplexed, she replied, "I am a Hindu."

"I didn't ask you about your religion, but who you are." More questions followed, but none satisfied Maharshi.

Confused, the woman went home. Constantly she had to think about Maharshi's question.

One day she decided to find the answer to the question of who she actually was herself. It was the beginning of a long search.

The Suffering Monk

An old monk came to an enlightened lama and told of his failed attempts to attain enlightenment.

"Gradually, I have reduced my possessions and given up more and more pleasures, thereby fighting my desires. I have fasted a lot, I stopped drinking alcohol, I have been a vegetarian for a long time, I don't smoke, and I even gave up coffee and tea. For years, I submitted to celibacy and chastised myself at regular intervals. Everything that was required of me, I did. I gave up everything, dropped every desire, every joy, every aspiration. I have suffered much, but enlightenment has not come. What else do you want me to do?"

The Lama replied, "Give up suffering!"

The Diamond

A dervish was on a journey. He reached the edge of a village and settled down under a tree to spend the night. Out of the blue, a villager came running to him.

"There you are!" the villager exclaimed excitedly. "Give me the precious stone!"

"What stone?" the dervish asked in surprise.

"Last night I had a vivid dream, which I remember clearly. In it, I dreamed that tonight, at nightfall, I would meet a man at the edge of the village who would give me a valuable stone. With the stone, I would be so rich that I would never have to work for money again."

The dervish reached into his pocket and pulled out a diamond. "Do you mean this stone?"

The villager could hardly believe his eyes. "Yes, exactly! That's it!"

"I found it a few days ago under a tree root that I used as a pillow. Here, take it." The dervish handed the diamond to the villager.

The latter could hardly believe his luck. The diamond was as big as his fist. It was probably the largest diamond in the world. He took the precious gem, thanked him, and ran away.

The next day, the man sold the diamond. He bought a villa, numerous cars, and much more. His possessions kept piling up and he never ran out of money. But this did not make him happier. The more he owned, the more unhappy he felt. It was as if he was missing something that money couldn't buy. The villager decided to seek out the dervish for help.

He found him in a nearby village and asked, "How can I possess the wealth that enabled you to so easily give away the diamond?"

Hakuin and a Samurai

A samurai once came to the Zen master Hakuin and asked, "Do heaven and hell exist, and if so, where do I find their entrance gates?"

As a warrior, he expected a crisp and clear answer and no spiritual gibberish.

"Who are you?" asked Hakuin.

"I am a samurai," he replied, although it was obvious from his clothing. As a samurai, he was valued and respected by all. As a warrior, he would not hesitate for a second to sacrifice his life for his lord.

Hakuin started laughing at him and said, "You, a samurai? You look like a beggar!"

The samurai's pride was hurt. After all, he was even a leader of the samurai. Impulsively, he unsheathed his sword to kill Hakuin on the spot.

"This is the Gate to Hell," Hakuin immediately replied to him. "With your sword, your anger, your ego, you open the gate."

The samurai immediately came to his senses and understood the words. He put his sword back into its scabbard.

Then Hakuin spoke, "Here the Gate to Heaven opens."

Show Me Your Hate

A disciple once came to Zen Master Bankei and said, "Master, I have a lot of hate inside me. Tell me, how can I get rid of it?"

"Show me your hate," Bankei demanded.

"I cannot show it to you. Right now I don't feel any hate."

"Then bring me your hate, if you have it."

"My hate always comes unexpectedly. The next time it happens, I will probably be far away from you and won't be able to bring it to you. I would lose it again on the way to you."

"If so, the hate has nothing to do with your true nature," Bankei explained. "If you keep losing it so easily, then there is no problem getting rid of it. The next time the hate comes, make your way to me. If you lose it on the way to me, set off again as soon as it comes again. Try this again and again. If you lose your hate every time, then you have found an effective means of getting rid of it. You can be sure of that."

The Wisdom of the Universe

A long time ago, the gods thought that it would be very bad if humankind, in their immaturity, found the wisdom of the universe. They agreed to hide the wisdom of the universe in a secret place. Humankind should find this wisdom only when they become mature enough for it.

One god proposed to hide the wisdom on the highest mountain on earth. But the gods quickly realized that humans would soon climb all the mountains and the wisdom would not be hidden safely enough on the mountaintop.

Another god suggested that this wisdom should be hidden in the deepest part of the ocean. But even there, the gods sensed the danger that humans would find the wisdom too soon.

Then the wisest of all gods then took the floor. "I know what to do. We will hide the wisdom of the universe inside humans themselves. They will search for it there only when they are mature enough as for this, they must go into their inner selves."

All the gods agreed that this was the best proposal. And so it happened that the wisdom of the universe was hidden inside humans themselves.

XIII

LOVE

Man loves not because it is his interest to love this or that,
but because love is the essence of his soul,
because he cannot but love.

– Leo Tolstoy

Unconditional Love

A woman went to a Kabbalist.

"I have pondered this for a long time and believe," she began, "that love is always the same, whether human or divine. Is this true?"

"No," replied the Kabbalist, "human and divine love are fundamentally different. When a man goes to work to earn money for the family, he expects in return that his wife will do the housework and raise the children. When a man helps his friend move, he expects his friend to help him in the future when he needs it. This kind of love is always connected with an expectation. It is a give and take." The Kabbalist pointed with both hands to the woman and then to himself as he continued. "I give you something; I expect you to give me something in return. In divine love, however, there is no such expectation. You help me move joyfully and of your own accord, without wanting anything in return. The characteristic of divine love is unconditional giving, unconditional love. This love unfolds only with complete selflessness."

The Perfect Woman

A long time ago, a swami sat in the temple with his disciples.

"Why didn't you ever get married?" one of the disciples asked.

"It wasn't exactly my choice. I once planned to marry. But I just wanted to marry the perfect woman. I wanted her to be beautiful, intelligent, and virtuous. So I spent many years looking for the perfect woman."

The students listened attentively.

"And did you find her?" one of the disciples finally asked.

"Yes, I did indeed find her," the swami replied. "She was perfect and I was overjoyed to have finally met her."

Other disciples asked what was on the tongue of everyone else, "Then why didn't you marry her?"

"I wanted to marry her, but she was looking for the perfect man."

Friendship

Buddha once told some children a story from one of his past lives. In that life, he had been a deer living in the forest. There was a lake the deer liked to drink from. A turtle lived in the lake and a magpie lived in the branches of a willow right next to the lake. The three animals were best friends.

One day a hunter noticed the tracks of the deer and followed them to the lake. There he set a trap made of rope and returned to his cabin at the edge of the forest. In the late afternoon, the deer came to the lake and the trap snapped shut. He began to scream loudly, so the turtle and the magpie immediately rushed to him. Together they wondered how to save the deer.

"Dear Tortoise, your jaw is very strong," said the magpie. "You can gnaw on these ropes to cut them. I will fly to the hunter and buy us more time by keeping him from coming back here."

At the hunter's hut, the magpie waited on a tree. When the hunter opened the door, the magpie flew with all its might into his face. The hunter staggered back to his hut feeling dazed. He lay down on the bed to recover. When he felt better, he took his knife and went out the back door. But the clever magpie had guessed he would do that! She was already waiting at the back of the hut and again flew into the hunter's face. This time, too, she hit him hard. The hunter fled back to his hut to think. A few hours passed and when the hunter next opened the door, he covered his face with a hat. When the magpie saw that she could not attack the hunter's face this time, she quickly flew back into the forest to warn her friends.

In the meantime, the turtle had almost gnawed through the last rope. Because she had been gnawing on the ropes all this time, her jaw was sore and bleeding. When the hunter appeared at the lake, the deer gave a violent jerk in fright, so that the rope broke and he was freed. Quickly the deer ran into the forest. The magpie flew high up to the willow. The poor turtle, however, was so exhausted from her efforts that she was completely at the mercy of the hunter.

The hunter was angry when he saw the deer escape. He threw the turtle into a jute bag and left it hanging on a branch. Then he took up the pursuit to finish off the deer. The deer, hiding behind a group of bushes, noticed the turtle's predicament. He thought, *My friends have put their lives on the line for me, now it's time to do the same for them.*

The deer stepped out from between the bushes so that the hunter could see him. As he did so, he pretended to stumble, as if he were very tired. Then he turned and walked slowly into the forest. The hunter thought that the deer had almost no strength left and decided to kill it with his knife.

He pursued the deer deeper and deeper into the forest. However, the deer managed to keep the hunter at a distance. In this way, he drove the hunter far away from the lake. Then suddenly the deer became faster and faster, and soon the hunter could no longer see him.

After covering his hoofprints, the deer ran back to the lake. With his antlers, he lifted the jute bag from the tree and placed it on the ground so that the turtle could get out. The magpie also flew over and joined its friends.

"Today, you both saved me from certain death!" the deer spoke to his friends. "But I'm afraid that the hunter will be here again soon. Magpie, fly to a safe place in the forest! Turtle, crawl back into the water, and hide there! I will run back to the forest!"

When the hunter returned to the lake, he found only his empty jute bag there. Disappointed, he picked it up, clutched his knife tightly, and set off back to his hut.

The Secret Prince

The inhabitants of the city were poor, bitter, and dissatisfied with their ruler, and the prince wanted to do something about it. He gathered the inhabitants in the marketplace to give them an important message. The crowd was curious and eager to hear what their ruler had to announce.

"My faithful inhabitants," the ruler began his speech, "I have secretly brought one of my children among you. Treat it well. If I learn that someone is making my child suffer or treating him unjustly, I will hold him accountable."

After this speech, the prince retired to his castle. The inhabitants were upset and wondered which child could be from the prince. Since they had no way of knowing, they henceforth began to treat all the children in the city as if each one was the princely child.

The years passed. The children grew up and had children of their own. The now-old prince watched with great interest and satisfaction the development in his city over all these years. The formerly poor and decaying city became a splendid city known far beyond its borders. Kindergartens, schools, hospitals, libraries, and even a university were built. More jobs were created and the inhabitants became wealthier and more educated.

What is Love?

A young girl asked her father if he could explain to her exactly what love is.

"No," he replied. "Since your mother and I got divorced, I don't know exactly what love is." The father's voice became depressed. "I thought what we had was love, but I was wrong."

Then the girl went to her mother and asked her the same question. But the mother could not answer the question either and referred to her ex-husband.

The next morning, the girl asked her kindergarten teacher if she knew what love is.

"Love is a gift," the kindergarten teacher replied kindly, "and when you grow up, I hope you will know it."

This answer did not satisfy the girl and she did not want to wait until she would grow up. She asked another question, "Can love be bought?"

"No, but there are people who think it can be."

At home, the girl asked her aunt if she knew what love is.

"Yes, I know," replied the aunt.

Then the girl became very bright-eyed and was eager to hear the answer.

"You can only get love if you also give love. Then your heart beats wildly and feels warm."

The girl asked what happens to the heart when you are alone.

"Then the heart feels alone, too."

The answer saddened the girl and she was still not satisfied. She desperately wanted to know what love is and asked other people, but no one had an answer she was happy with.

When the weekend came, the girl visited her grandma, who had been happily married for many years. She thought that her grandma must know what love is and asked her the question.

Her grandma smiled and, without answering, went into the house. She came back with a small old treasure chest. "Look inside and you will find the answer to your question."

The girl was very curious, carefully opened the chest, and found a mirror inside.

"Look at yourself," Grandma urged her. "You have love inside you. Your heart shines in the most beautiful colors and you may always love yourself just as you are." Grandma smiled. "When you love yourself, you radiate that love. And with that radiance, you attract people who will love you. So remember this: you always carry love within you."

The Brahmin and His Nephew

The nephew of a Brahmin had taken over as treasurer of a small village. However, the villagers did not miss the nephew's lavish lifestyle. Since he had taken over as treasurer, he had been spending far too much money, including on private matters. The villagers were worried about the future of their village and contacted the Brahmin. The latter immediately agreed to pay a visit to his nephew.

When the Brahmin knocked on his door, the treasurer was delighted to meet his uncle. He had not seen him for years. He invited his uncle to spend the night. The Brahmin spent the whole night in meditation and when he was about to leave in the morning, he said, "I seem to be getting old, my hands are shaking so. Would you please help me tie the straps of my sandals?"

The nephew willingly helped him.

"Thank you," said the Brahmin. "You see, one grows older and more feeble day by day. Take good care of yourself."

He said goodbye to his nephew without mentioning the real reason for his visit. But since that day, the nephew's lavish life had come to an end.

In Exile

Once there lived a prince named Rahul. Rahul had a big heart. He always helped the poor and needy and never hesitated to give away his property to them. His wife Esha was as charitable as he was. She knew how much it made her husband happy to help others. And so she never complained when he gave away his possessions. Rahul and Esha had a son, Sunil, and a daughter, Manju.

During a famine, Prince Rahul asked his father for permission to distribute food and clothing from the royal storehouse to the poor. The king agreed. However, the famine lasted for a long time, so that the supplies were soon exhausted. This worried some of the king's ministers. They made plans to stop the prince from giving away anymore. First, they told the king that the prince's indiscriminate giving would mean the ruin of the kingdom. They told him that the prince had even given away one of the valuable royal elephants.

The influence of the ministers had an effect. The king became worried and was persuaded to banish his only son to the distant mountains. There he was to experience firsthand the hardships of the simple life. Thus it came to pass that Rahul, Esha, and the two children were exiled.

On their journey, they met a poor beggar. The prince gave him his expensive jacket without hesitation. They met other needy people on their journey. Esha gave away her royal coat and even the children donated their capes to the poor. It was not long before they had given away all their possessions. Finally, the prince also gave the carriage along with horses. They continued their journey on foot. Without any regret, they walked until they reached the mountains. They walked without worry and were in good spirits.

But there was still a long distance ahead of them and the feet of Rahul and Esha, who carried their children in their arms, were swollen and bloody. When they finally arrived in the mountains, they found an abandoned hut. The hut once belonged to a hermit. They cleaned it and made beds out of small branches and leaves. They fed mainly on fruits they found in the forest. The children learned to distinguish poisonous from edible food, gathered fruits, washed their clothes in a mountain spring, and helped with gardening. The couple taught the children. They used large leaves as paper and large thorns as pens.

They made the best of the difficult circumstances and were content. Two years had passed when a stranger kidnapped the children while the parents were gathering fruit in the forest. The prince and his wife searched the forest and nearby villages for days, but their search was in vain.

Having lost hope of still finding the children, they returned to their hut. They still hoped that the children had returned on their own in the meantime. To their surprise, they found a royal messenger waiting for them. From him they learned that Sunil and Manju were safe and sound in the king's palace.

"Tell me, how did our children get back to the palace?" asked Rahul the messenger.

"A few days ago, one of the king's cooks saw the children at the market where they were to be sold," the messenger reported. "She immediately recognized your children and quickly ran to the palace to tell them about it. The king had the children and the merchant brought them to the palace. Despite their tattered clothes and dirty faces, the king immediately recognized his grandchildren. He saw how big they had grown in two years. He felt how much he had missed them and you. The king asked the merchant where he got the children and how much he would sell them for. Before the merchant could answer, a minister said that the girl would cost one thousand gold pieces and the boy one hundred. Everyone – including the merchant and the children – was very surprised at these words. The king asked why the girl was so much more expensive than the boy. The minister answered that the king obviously values girls more than boys. He never punishes the princess or scolds her. He also always treats the ladies-in-waiting and maids in the palace with kindness and respect. But the king has only one son, the heir to the throne. And yet the king has exiled him far from home." The messenger paused briefly and took a sip of water before continuing. "The king had understood and was moved to tears. He learned that the merchant had bought your children from another man in the mountains. Your father paid the merchant and had the kidnapper arrested. From your children the king learned how you had fared in the mountains. He ordered me to bring his son and daughter-in-law back to the capital."

After the messenger told Rahul and Esha everything, they returned to the palace together. From that time on, the king appreciated his son much more than before. He also generously supported his efforts to alleviate the suffering of the poor.

XIV
PERCEIVED REALITY

Although they are seeing,
they do not see,
though hearing,
they do not hear,
and neither do they understand.

– Jesus

Conversation in the Womb

A woman was carrying twins in her womb. She was already in the last third of pregnancy and the following conversation took place in her womb.

"Do you actually believe in life after birth?" the first twin asked the second.

"Yes, I do believe in that. This place is where we grow and prepare for life after birth. Don't you?"

"No, I don't believe in such fairy tales. What is it supposed to look like anyway, life after birth?"

"I don't know exactly. But I think it will be brighter than here. And maybe we will walk around with our arms and legs, take water through our nose and food with our mouth."

"What nonsense! Why would we eat with our mouths when we have this perfectly fine umbilical cord that serves us all the food we need? And how are we supposed to walk around anyway? The space here is way too cramped."

"It sounds strange but it'll all just be a little different."

"Where do you get such strange ideas?" asked the first twin. "No one has ever come back after birth to prove it. With birth, our existence will be over."

"Of course, I don't know in detail what life after birth will look like and what it will be like," the second admitted, "but we will finally get to see our mother. She'll take care of us all right."

This statement made the first twin angry. "Mother? Don't tell me you believe in a mother too! Where is she supposed to be?"

"Well, here! All around us. We live in her. After all, we can't be without her!"

The first twin already became slightly aggressive. "Nonsense!" he retorted. "If a mother existed, I would surely have noticed. So she must not exist either."

"You need to pay better attention. When we're quiet, you can hear her voice and feel her caressing our world."

Plato's Cave

Plato's Allegory of the Cave is the most famous allegory in ancient philosophy. He described it in the seventh book of his masterpiece *The Republic* in the form of a dialogue between Socrates and Glaucon.

Socrates: Now understand, by means of the following allegory, the difference between the state of our nature when it is in possession of full education and when it lacks it. Imagine an underground cave-like dwelling with a long upward entrance. With people who have sat all their lives with their backs to the entrance, with their legs and necks bound so that they cannot turn around. The light comes from a fire burning far above and behind them. Between the fire and the prisoners is a wall.

Glaucon: This is all before my eyes.

Socrates: Along this wall – you have to imagine it now further – puppeteers carry all kinds of objects which cast shadows on the wall in front of the bound prisoners. Some of the carriers utter sounds, while others are silent.

Glaucon: It's a strange image and strange prisoners you're telling of.

Socrates: They are like us. For do you think that such people have seen anything of themselves other than the shadows cast by the fire on the side of the cave facing them?

Glaucon: How would that be possible, if they have to keep their heads motionless throughout their lives?

Socrates: And what about the objects that are carried by?

Glaucon: They saw only shadows of them, too.

Socrates: If they were able to discuss things with one another, don't you think they would name things correctly?

Glaucon: Necessarily.

Socrates: And what if the cave also had an echo from the side facing them? Whenever one of the puppeteers made a sound as he passed by. Do you think they would then believe that something other than the passing shadow was making the sound?

Glaucon: No, by Zeus, I don't.

Socrates: Then such people would certainly claim that truth is nothing but the shadow of artificial objects.

Glaucon: Most likely.

Socrates: Now consider what their liberation and healing from bonds and folly would be like if something like this were to happen to them. Take one of these prisoners who is freed and is suddenly forced to stand up. He must now turn his neck, look up at the light and walk on his own. With all the pain he has because he is dazzled and cannot see the things whose shadows he saw before. What do you suppose he'd say if someone were to tell him that before he saw silly nothings? Whereas now he sees more correctly because he is a little nearer to what is. And if someone showed him each of the objects that were previously passed along the wall by the puppeteers and forced him to answer questions about what they are? Don't you suppose he would be perplexed and not know what they are? Would he believe that what he saw before was truer than what is now shown?

Glaucon: Yes, by far.

Socrates: And if he were now forced to direct his gaze to the light itself. Would his eyes then hurt? Would he turn again to what is known to him and what he can recognize? And consider it more certain than what is outside the cave?

Glaucon: He would.

Socrates: And if someone were to force him away from the dwelling place, up the rough, steep path? He would not be let go until he was brought to the light of the sun. Would he not then be distressed and angry at being dragged like this? And if he came to the light, would he not be blinded by all the splendor? By all that is now presented to him as the only true thing? Would he even be able to recognize it?

Glaucon: No, he wouldn't, at least not right away.

Socrates: Then he will probably have to get used to it, if he wants to see what is up there. Beyond his previous dwelling place. First he would recognize the shadows most easily. Then the images of the people, the other things in the water and later the things themselves. And from there he will see the things in the sky and the sky itself. And this more easily at night in the light of the stars and the moon than during the day when he looked at the sun and sunlight.

Glaucon: Yes, of course.

Socrates: Then he will probably finally be able to recognize the sun – not its reflection in the water, but the sun itself in its own region – and see what it looks like.

Glaucon: Necessarily.

Socrates: And after that, he would already be able to conclude that this is the source of the seasons and the years. And that the sun is the administrator of all things in the visible place and in some way the

cause of all those things that he and his company-
ions saw in the dwelling.

Glaucon: Obviously, he would come to this understanding
in such a sequence of stages.

Socrates: What then? If he remembers his first home and the
wisdom there, and his fellow prisoners during that
time? Don't you think he would rejoice in the
change and pity those left behind in the cave?

Glaucon: Certainly.

Socrates: Now also consider the following: If such a man
came down again and sat down in his old place in
the cave, if he suddenly came out of the sun,
would not his eyes be infected with darkness?

Glaucon: Very much so.

Socrates: And if he had to compete once again with these
eternally bound ones? To form a judgment on
these shadows while his vision is still clouded and
before his eyes have recovered? If the time it
would take him to get used to them were not short
at all? Would they not then laugh at him and say
that he had gone up and come back with spoiled
eyes and that it was not even worth going up? And
if the others somehow got hold of the man who
was actually trying to free them? Wouldn't they
kill him then?

Glaucon: There is no doubt about that.

Socrates: This allegory, my dear Glaucon – you must understand in its full scope as follows. Compare the
world that reveals itself through our normal sense
of sight with the underground cave-like dwelling
and the light of the fire in it with the power of the
sun. While the ascent and the seeing of what is
above is the elevation of the soul up into the realm

of what is only thinkable. Thus you get a real idea of my perception, since you wish to hear it.

Allegory of the Cave by Gregory the Great

Around the year 600 A.D., Gregory the Great wrote a short allegory of the cave.

An expectant mother is thrown into prison. The newborn is raised inside the prison walls. When the mother tells the child about the sun, the moon, and the stars, about mountains and rivers, about flying birds, and about galloping horses, the boy feels helpless. Growing up in prison, the boy knows only darkness. He hears about objects, but he has to doubt the existence of trees, mountains, and animals, because he has never known the world through his own experience.

It is the same with human beings. Because they are born blind and must live in the earthly world, they have doubts about the existence of supreme invisible things.

Tolstoy's Parable of Reality

Another parable about perceived reality was described by Leo Tolstoy in his 1894 book, *The Kingdom of God Is Within You.*

One summer day, a doctor, a specialist in mental health, wanted to leave the asylum. The residents accompanied him to the street door.

"Come for a walk in the town with me?" the doctor suggested to his patients.

The residents agreed, and a small group followed the doctor. But the further they walked along the street, where healthy people moved freely, the more timid they became. They pressed closer and closer to the doctor and prevented him from walking. At last they all begged him to take them back to the asylum – to their bleak but familiar life with their keepers, straitjackets, and solitary cells.

The Temple of a Thousand Mirrors

A long time ago, there was a temple that consisted of a large room with one-thousand mirrors. It was located high up a mountain and the sight of it was impressive.

A dog spotted the temple from afar and ran there. When he entered the temple, he saw thousands of dogs. He was frightened, began to growl, and bared his teeth. At the same time, the thousands of dogs growled at him and bared their teeth. Full of fear, the dog left the temple and ran for his life. He began to believe that the whole world would consist of aggressive dogs.

Not long after, another dog entered the temple of a thousand mirrors and saw thousands of dogs. The dog was happy, he started wagging his tail and jumping around in joy. The thousands of dogs in the temple did the same. After some time, he left the temple and was convinced that the world was made up of friendly dogs that were well disposed toward him.

A Disagreement of the Senses

The eye spoke to the other sense organs, "Over there I see a mountain. On top of it is bright white snow. Isn't that beautiful?"

The ear listened and said, "Where is the mountain? I don't hear one."

The hand groped around and asked, "I can't grasp it. Where is the mountain you see there?"

The nose stated, "I don't smell anything. There is no mountain."

The tongue agreed. Since it tasted no mountain, there could be none.

Misunderstood by the other sense organs, the eye turns away from the mountain and looks across the land. Meanwhile, the other organs discuss the eye and its strange ideas about the mountain. They come to the conclusion that there is something wrong with the eye.

What Are the People Like?

A man was looking for a new house and went to the magistrate.

"I am thinking of buying a house in this village," the man explained. "But first I would like to know what the people are like here. As a magistrate, surely you can tell me something about the people here in the village?"

The magistrate asked a counter question, "What are the people like in your present village?"

"Oh, don't ask. They are all liars and cheats. They are quite unfriendly people! That is why I want to move to another village."

"The people here are the same."

Thereupon the man said goodbye and continued his search in another village.

A few weeks later, another stranger came to the village. He also went to the magistrate. "I am thinking of moving to this beautiful village," the man began the conversation. "Can you tell me something about the people who live here?"

Again, the magistrate asked a counter question, "What are the people like in your present village?"

"Oh, I'm glad you asked. They are friendly, helpful, and good-natured. All of them are especially kind people whom I will miss very much."

"That's just the way people are here in our village."

The Ax Thief

A woodcutter went into his garden after breakfast and noticed that his ax was no longer in its usual place. In despair, he looked around but could not find it. He became angry and suspected that his neighbor had stolen the ax.

When the neighbor passed by the woodcutter's house, the woodcutter's suspicions were confirmed: The neighbor behaved like an ax thief, moved like an ax thief, and spoke like an ax thief.

Late in the afternoon, the woodcutter went to his wood supply and found his ax on the tree stump where he always chopped the firewood. He had simply forgotten to put it in its usual place the day before.

In the evening, he sat on his porch and watched his neighbor walk by. And he observed that his behavior was not that of an ax thief, his walk was not that of an ax thief, and his words did not sound like those of an ax thief.

Does God Exist?

A man came to the Tathagata and asked him, "Does God exist?"

"No, he does not," replied the Tathagata.

A few days later, another man came and asked the same question, "Does God exist?"

"Yes, he does exist!" the Tathagata answered this time.

Later, a third man came and also asked if God exists. The Tathagata began to meditate. The man followed suit. After a few hours, both opened their eyes again and the man devoutly touched the Tathagata's feet.

"Many thanks for answering my question," he said.

Ananda, the servant of the Tathagata, was present the whole time.

"All three men came to you with the same question," he said to the Tathagata. "To the first man you answered 'No', to the second 'Yes'. To the third you said nothing, but meditate-ed. Why did you give these men three different answers?"

The Tathagata replied, "The first firmly believed in God, so I had to take away his illusion. The second was an atheist, so I had to destroy that illusion for him as well. The third was a seeker who really had the question on his mind, so I could really answer him."

Five Blind Advisors

One day, the king sent five blind advisors on a journey to Africa to find out exactly what an elephant is. Once there, the blind advisors were led to an elephant. They stood around the animal and tried to get a picture of the elephant by feeling it.

Back in the kingdom, they went together to the king. The first advisor, who had stood by the animal's head and felt its trunk, reported, "An elephant is like a long arm."

The second advisor, who had felt the elephant's ear, contradicted the first advisor: "No, the elephant is like a large fan!"

The third advisor said, "Not at all! An elephant is like a thick pillar." He had felt one of the elephant's legs.

"That's not true either, it feels like a small string with a tuft of hair at the end!" replied the advisor who had grasped the elephant's tail.

And finally, the fifth advisor reported to his king, "Well, I say an elephant is like a huge mass, with curves and a few bristles on it." He had felt the torso of the animal.

The five advisors could not agree on what an elephant really is and a heated discussion ensued. They had begun to fear the king's wrath, when he suddenly spoke up with a smile.

"I thank you, for I now know what an elephant is: an elephant is an animal with a trunk that is like a long arm, with ears that are like fans, with legs that are like strong pillars, with a tail that is like a small string with a tuft of hair on it, and with a torso that is like a large mass with curves and a few bristles."

The advisors lowered their heads in shame after realizing that each of them had only felt a part of the elephant and had not understood the whole.

Good and Bad People

In ancient India, a guru had two fundamentally different disciples, Amal and Himal. While Amal was always optimistic, Himal was always pessimistic.

The guru said to Himal, "Go on a journey and find a good person. Once you find him, bring him to us."

Himal packed some things for the journey and left. After months, he finally returned to his guru unaccompanied.

"My guru, I could not find a single good person in the whole world," Himal reported. "Everywhere I saw only bad people."

The guru then said to Amal, "Go on the journey and find a bad person. Once you find him, bring him to us."

Amal packed some things for the journey and left. He too returned to his guru after a few months. Like Himal before, Amal also came unaccompanied.

"My guru, I could not find a single bad person. Everywhere I saw only good people."

Although the two disciples encountered the same people on their long journey, their statements contradicted each other.

The guru clarified: "You see in the world the reflection of your own mind. Therefore, the world appears full of good people to Amal and full of bad people to Himal. As your mind is set, so is its outlook."

XV
HOPE

Our deepest fear is not that we are inadequate,
our deepest fear is that we are powerful beyond measure.

It is our light, not our darkness,
that most frightens us.

We ask ourselves, who am I to be brilliant,
gorgeous, talented and fabulous?

Actually, who are you not to be?
You are a child of God.
Your playing small doesn't serve the world.

There's nothing enlightened about shrinking
so that other people won't feel insecure around you.

We were born to make manifest the glory of God that is with-
in us. It's not just in some of us, it's in everyone.

And as we let our own light shine, we consciously give
other people permission to do the same.

As we are liberated from our own fear,
our presence automatically liberates others.

– Nelson Mandela

Perseverance

A woman was in a life crisis. Her employment was terminated. She was also recently divorced, and seriously ill. She had such great plans for the future. She wanted to be happy, meet new friends and acquaintances, and stand on her own two feet again financially. She went to an old sage. From some acquaintances the woman heard that he was not a charlatan, but had already helped many people.

When she reached him, she described her life crisis. "Can you please give me even one single reason why I should still be optimistic?" she asked.

The sage was silent at first, got up and went into his garden. The woman followed him.

He told her a story: "Do you see the maple and the princess trees? I sowed the seeds of both trees on the same day. The two had the same starting conditions from the beginning. I provided enough water and light. And after a short time the princess tree grew out of the ground. After one year it has already reached a proud height of twenty feet. Meanwhile, the maple could not be seen. But I did not give up on it. In the second year, the princess tree continued to grow in height. However, there was still no sign of the maple. And yet I did not give up and continued to nurture the princess tree and the place where I put the maple seed in the ground. The next years showed the same result: while the princess tree developed splendidly, there was no trace of the maple. But I did not give up hope and continued to take care of both trees. It wasn't until the fifth year that a tiny, inconspicuous maple shoot came up out of the ground. I almost overlooked it. But after just one year it had reached a height of three feet. So it had taken a full five years for the maple to grow strong enough roots and come to the surface. Now many years have passed in the meantime. As you can see, the maple is now twice the size of the princess tree. Even if you look back on your low points where it seems you have made no progress, in reality, you have grown roots during this time, just like the maple. Your time will come, you must not bury your head in the sand. Don't compare yourself with others, because we all have our individual destinies – just as the princess tree has a different one than the maple. You will grow."

The woman had listened to him attentively. "How high do you want me to grow?" she asked.

The sage asked her a counter question, "How high does the maple grow?"

"As high as it can?"

"That's right. So have some patience, even if it's not easy for you in your current situation. Just give yourself the time you need and grow as high as you can. There are still many good things waiting for you."

The Goat in the Well

A goat had fallen into a dried-up well in the middle of a village. The farmer became aware of it because of the loud screaming and, with the other villagers, tried to get the goat out of the well. They tried numerous rescue options, but none had worked.

And so, the men decided to let the goat die in the well. The well had not been in use for a long time and was to be filled in anyway. The men shoveled the gravel and rubble lying around into the well in order to put the old goat out of its misery more quickly and bury it immediately in the well. The goat realized what was going on and cried for its life.

After a while, it became surprisingly quiet in the well. The farmer took a look into the well to see if the goat had already been buried and was astonished at what he saw. The goat was not covered at all. It shook every shovelful of gravel and rubble off of itself and trampled on it, causing the ground beneath its feet to rise ever higher. When the villagers saw this, they diligently continued to pour gravel and debris into the well until the goat left under its own power.

A Heavy Load

At an oasis, a young palm tree was growing. A malicious man passed by, saw the small palm tree, took a heavy stone, and placed it on the palm tree. Laughing mischievously, he left the oasis again. The little palm tree tried in vain to shake off the stone. After a while, it realized that it could not shake off the extra weight and focused on its roots. With these, it penetrated deeper into the earth in order to gain a more stable hold and be able to lift the additional load. It succeeded so well that its roots spread vigorously and even reached the groundwater.

Thus, despite the heavy weight of the stone, the small palm grew over the years to become the largest palm tree in the oasis. When the culprit came back to the oasis after some years, he expected to see a crippled or dead palm tree. He could not believe his eyes when he saw that the palm was so strong and tall, despite the stone on its crown.

The Advent Wreath

The four candles of an Advent wreath were all burning. When no one was in the room, the first candle sighed, "I represent peace, but because people don't keep the peace, I shine fainter and fainter." A breeze soon extinguished the first candle.

The second candle flickered and said, "I represent faith. But my flame is also getting smaller because people are not interested in attaining higher knowledge." Its flame also went out shortly after.

Then the third candle spoke up. "I represent love, but I too am at the end of my rope. People have become far too selfish and neglectful of their fellow human beings." So the flame of the third candle also went out.

Shortly after, a child came into the living room and became very sad that only one candle was still burning. She began to cry.

"Don't be sad" the fourth candle then said to her. "As long as I burn, we can relight the other candles. I represent hope!"

The child took the candle in her hand and with its flame lit the other three candles, so that the whole Advent wreath shone once again.

XVI

HABIT

A man can only think in his worn grooves,
and unless he has the courage to fill up these
and make new ones for himself
he must perforce travel on the old lines.

– Mahatma Koot' Hoomi Lal Singh

The Frog in the Pot

A woman was sitting on her porch on the shore of a small pond. She was admiring nature and enjoying the silence. Then she saw a frog and caught it. She went to the kitchen, filled a pot with water, and heated it. When the water boiled, she wanted to throw the frog in alive. But the frog made a desperate leap out of the pot, hopped out of the hut, and disappeared into the undergrowth.

The next day, the woman was enjoying the afternoon again on her porch, having done all the household chores. There she saw another frog. Again she caught it and brought it to the kitchen. She filled the pot with water and put it on the stove. While the water was still cold, she added the frog. To her surprise, the woman noticed that the frog did not try to escape from the pot. The water got warmer and warmer until it finally got hot and began to boil. But the frog stayed in the pot the whole time. Even when the water became dangerously hot, it made no attempt to escape from the life-threatening situation. So it happened that the frog died in the pot.

While the woman was eating the meal, she wondered why the frog had not jumped out of the increasingly hot water to save itself.

One Man on an Island

A man lived alone on a very small island. One day he felt an earthquake shaking the ground. He watched as a piece of the coast broke off and sank into the ocean. He wondered what he should do. But shortly after, the quake stopped and he decided to wait and see.

A few days later, during his daily walk around the island, he noticed that another piece of the island had been swallowed by the ocean. Again, he wondered if he should do something. But he decided to wait and see. After all, most of the island was still there and the earthquake had fortunately spared his house.

In the evening he was preparing his dinner at the campfire and heard a loud noise. He went to check and found that once again a part of the island had sunk into the ocean.

At first, he was startled and wondered if he should do something. But then he decided to wait again. In this way, days and weeks passed until finally the entire island sank into the ocean.

The man was floating on the open sea. Clinging to a log, he thought just before drowning, *Maybe I should have done something after all.*

The Elephant in the Circus

An elephant was born in a circus and immediately chained to a tree by its hind leg. Thus, he could only move within a certain radius around the tree. This circle defined its world. The elephant was still too weak to free itself from the chains. Every attempt – and it made countless attempts – ended painfully and unsuccessfully. Eventually, the young elephant resigned itself to the hopeless situation. It understood that it was fine in its radius and that every attempt to leave the radius was associated with pain.

Years passed and the elephant was no longer chained to the tree. It had grown big and strong. With its present strength, it could have freed itself from its chains at that time. Nevertheless, it had never left its former range of motion and remained near the tree.

The Centipede

A centipede walked past a frog. The frog watched the centipede's thousand feet and wondered how he did it. It was not easy for the frog to walk on four feet.

"It's remarkable how you move so smoothly with your thousand feet," he said to the centipede. "How do you know when to put which foot where in such a short time? That would completely overwhelm me."

"I've been walking all my life, but have never really thought about it," the centipede replied in amazement. "It happens automatically, after all."

The centipede began to think and it now also seemed incredibly complex to him too. For the first time he realized how complicated it was to move with a thousand feet. For several minutes he stood there thinking about which foot he should move first. Suddenly, he realized he couldn't move at all.

About Tradition

A newly married couple had just moved into their first house and the wife decided to braise a leg of lamb to mark the occasion. She cut the leg in half and put it in the casserole dish. Her husband saw this and asked why she hadn't put the whole leg in the pot.

"That's how my mother always did it," she answered him.

On the next occasion, the man asked his mother-in-law why the leg had to be cut in half and received the same answer: "That's the way my mother always did it."

Both answers did not satisfy him, so he asked his wife's grandmother why the leg had to be cut in half.

"Oh, there's a very simple reason for that," the grandmother answered him. "My casserole dish was too small back then, so a whole leg didn't fit in it, so I always had to cut it in half."

XVII
HUMAN EVOLUTION

A stone becomes a plant,
a plant an animal,
an animal a man,
a man a spirit,
and a spirit a god.

– Kabbalistic axiom

The Prodigal Son

Jesus once told of a wealthy father who had two sons. The younger son asked, "Father, please give me the inheritance that is rightfully mine."

The father agreed and gave him the belongings. The son went to a distant town with many temptations to which he succumbed. He quickly squandered his entire inheritance.

Then a great famine came upon that city. Without any financial means, he began to starve and decided to work for a living. He began to work as a laborer for one of the towns-people, tending the sows. In his need, he longed to eat the pods that the sows were eating, but no one gave them to him. Then something dawned on him and he said to himself, *My father has many laborers who have bread in abundance, while I perish and starve here! I will return to my father and confess to him that I have sinned and squandered my inheritance.* In his insight, he also decided that he was no longer worthy to be the son of his virtuous father. He wanted to be equal to the other laborers upon his return.

As he approached his hometown, his father caught sight of him and ran to his son, embracing and kissing him.

"Father, I have sinned and squandered my inheritance," spoke the son, visibly astonished by his father's reception. "I am no longer worthy to be your son. I want to work for you as a laborer."

"Quickly, bring the best clothes and shoes for my lost son," the father ordered his servants. "My son was dead and has come back to life; he was lost and has been found. Today we will celebrate the return of my son. Slaughter the fatted calf for this!"

When the elder son returned home from the field, he heard the celebration.

"What's going on here?" the elder asked one of the servants. "Why are people singing and dancing?"

"Your brother has returned home," the servant replied. "Your father has had the calf slaughtered in his honor and ordered a celebration."

The elder son became angry and did not want to take part in the celebration. When his father noticed this, he went out to talk to him.

"Father, for so many years I have faithfully worked here with you and have not violated any of your commandments," said the elder son. "Never have you slaughtered a calf for me or held such a celebration for me. But for your younger son, who had squandered your possessions on prostitutes, you slaughtered the fatted calf."

"My son, you have always remained with me and everything that belongs to me also belongs to you. You should not be angry with your brother, but rejoice: For your brother was dead and is alive again; he was lost and now is found."

Two Wolves

An old Cherokee chief and his son were sitting by a campfire. Silently, both gazed into the flames until the chief spoke up.

"You know, my son, we humans carry two wolves in our heart. All of us. And between these two wolves is an incessant battle."

Both looked silently into the flames again until the chief continued speaking.

"The one wolf is black. He embodies the dark side of life: egoism, envy, hatred, lies, illness, and pain. The other wolf is white. He stands for everything good in life: altruism, love, peace, gratitude, health, and honesty. For as long as humans have existed, this battle of the two wolves has raged."

The chief stopped speaking. His son looked into the campfire and thought about the words.

"Which wolf is winning?" he asked after a while. "The black wolf or the white wolf?"

"The one you feed wins."

Insatiability

A man was sitting all alone in the forest. He looked so sad that all the animals took pity on him. They gathered around him and said, "You look so sad. You can wish for anything from us to make you feel better."

"I want to have good eyes," the man replied.

"You shall have my eyes," the eagle decided.

"I want to be strong," the man continued to demand, to which the bear replied, "You shall be as strong as I am."

"Besides, I want to know the secrets of nature," the man finally said.

"I will teach them to you," the snake proclaimed.

And so all the animals helped the man. After acquiring all that the animals could give him, the man left the forest.

"Now the man can do everything and knows everything we can do and know," the fox spoke to the other animals. "Suddenly I feel scared."

"Yes, but he is no longer so sad," said the rabbit. "We helped him."

"No, I saw an emptiness in the man," replied the fox. "It was so big that it couldn't be satisfied. That's why he was sad and will continue to be sad. He wants more and more, and one day the time will come when there is nothing more to take."

Nails in the Fence

A little boy was always losing his temper. His parents wondered what they could do about it. Then the father had an idea: he gave his son a hammer and a box full of nails. Every time he lost his temper, he was to hammer a nail into the garden fence instead of taking out his anger on other people or objects.

The boy followed his instructions. On the first day alone he hammered twenty nails into the fence. The days passed and he hammered more nails into the fence, and the nails in the box became fewer and fewer. He began to realize that it was easier to not lose his temper than to pound nails into the fence.

The day came when the boy no longer lost his temper at all, and he proudly told his father. His father, very pleased with his son's progress, gave him a nail puller and instructed him to pull a nail out of the fence for every day he kept his temper. Days, weeks, and months passed. Every day, the boy pulled a nail from the fence until he had eventually removed all the nails from the fence. The father went to the fence with his son.

"You did well, my son," said the father. "I am proud of you. Do you see all the holes in the fence? The fence is not what it used to be. Remember this the next time you do or say something to others in anger. Your words may leave a scar, just as the nails left holes in the fence. Even if you apologize and feel remorse afterward, the wound is still there."

The Small Wave

A little wave was bouncing up and down on the sea having a great time. She enjoyed the great weather, the fish, the birds, and the fresh air. Then she noticed the other waves in front of her. She saw them crashing on the shore and panicked.

"Oh no, that's terrible!" she exclaimed, "and that's about to happen to me too."

A larger wave approached her from behind. "Why do you look so scared?" the larger wave asked.

"Don't you see what's going to happen to us? We're about to crash on the shore!"

"Do not be afraid. All waves are created and dissolve periodically. In essence, you are not a wave but a part of the ocean."

Passing Through

A tourist set out for the distant Himalayas. After a long and exhausting journey, he passed a cave where there was a yogini. Astonished, he noticed that the woman had nothing with her except her robe and a beggar's bowl.

"Do you live here?" he asked her.

When the yogini answered in the affirmative, the tourist asked the next question. "But why do you have so few things?"

"Why do you have so few items with you?" the yogini asked in turn.

"Well, I am just passing through."

The yogini smiled and said, "So am I."